THE
PIRATE'S
WIFE

Also by Daphne Palmer Geanacopoulos

The Pirate Next Door: The Untold Story of Eighteenth Century Pirates' Wives, Families and Communities

THE
PIRATE'S
WIFE

The Remarkable
True Story
of Sarah Kidd

DAPHNE PALMER GEANACOPOULOS

HANOVER
SQUARE
PRESS

HANOVER
SQUARE
PRESS™

Recycling programs
for this product may
not exist in your area.

ISBN-13: 978-1-335-42984-1

The Pirate's Wife

Hanover Square Press
22 Adelaide St. West, 41st Floor
Toronto, Ontario M5H 4E3, Canada
HanoverSqPress.com
BookClubbish.com

Printed in U.S.A.

To the memory of my grandmother, Juliette Marie Wehrmann Palmer

Contents

Prologue

Sarah Kidd lay in a weakened state in the bedroom of her Manhattan mansion. A highly contagious lethal disease raged through the colony striking young and old, rich or poor, Black or white. It was September 12, 1744, and the seventy-four-year-old Sarah had first taken to her bed to get warm under her soft quilts and to rest her head on the goose down pillows. Then the chills, fever, and fatigue set in. She was nearly certain she had contracted the deadly disease everyone called diphtheria. As a precaution, she asked her family and friends to stay at a safe distance. She arranged for soft foods and a soothing drink made from the medicinal herbs in her garden to be left outside her bedroom door.

Her mind wandered in a fever-induced haze. She closed her eyes and remembered herself in another time and place. She was a young woman with her husband, Captain William Kidd, on his pirate ship, the *Saint Antonio*, a vessel laden with gold, silver, and jewels. As his closest confidant, she learned that he'd buried some of his stolen treasure for safekeeping, and he described to her where it was hidden. She was not to tell a soul. For more than forty years, since his death in 1701, Sarah, the pirate's wife, kept his secret safe. Not even her five children knew. She alluded to it in her will, noting that she had assets in "the City of New York and elsewhere." She did not identify "elsewhere." Sarah worried about the consequences if her children were caught with stolen pirate loot. Her strong instincts told her it was best to leave well enough alone.

As she thought back over her life, not all of her memories were fond ones, especially the time when she was a pirate's wife. But now the memory of the hardships and heartbreak had softened and Sarah wouldn't have traded it for anything. She felt proud, very proud, to have been a pirate's wife and she wore the title as a badge of honor.

Sarah repeated a prayer as her condition worsened: "Almighty God, have mercy on my soul and pardon and forgive me all my sins & offences so that I may after this Miserable Life arise with our savior Jesus Christ."[1] She became delirious from the fever and shook uncontrollably. The sheets were soaked with her perspiration. Still, the thought of that secret weighed on her, as well-kept secrets do.

As she prayed for forgiveness she may have thought it was time to identify "elsewhere" to her three children who paced downstairs in the sitting room.

It wasn't long before Sarah developed a sore throat that felt like a razor when she swallowed. She tried to speak, but it hurt so much she could only whisper. Her daughter, Elizabeth Kidd Troup, peeked through the keyhole to check on Sarah. The once vigorous woman now appeared very small among the many furnishings and tasseled curtains. She looked pale in her white cotton bedclothes and so frail lying on her side facing the door. Elizabeth saw her mother's lips moving, mouthing words, but she could not hear her. She strained through the keyhole to hear what she might be whispering. Elizabeth called for her brothers, William and Henry, who had stepped outside on the front stoop that faced the harbor. The cry of the seagulls seemed to signal the alarm. Elizabeth told them to hurry. Each took a turn at the keyhole looking and listening. Sarah's breathing was loud and strained as she gasped for air. The three of them looked at each other with tears in their eyes when the room fell quiet. There was not a sound, not even a whisper.

For over three hundred years treasure hunters have scoured the North American eastern seaboard trying to find where "elsewhere" is. That secret is with Sarah, buried in the churchyard of Trinity Church Wall Street in Manhattan.

1

Sarah's New World

The lookout on the ship carrying passengers from England in 1684 spotted the bustling seaport at the tip of Manhattan first. On board was fourteen-year-old Sarah Bradley, her father, Captain Samuel Bradley, and her two younger brothers, Samuel Jr. and Henry. Sarah was weary from the voyage, an arduous weeks-long journey across the Atlantic. She had packed her bags with her most treasured possessions and left her home in England at the insistence of her father.[1] From the deck of the ship she glimpsed her new homeland for the first time—the former Dutch colony of New Netherland, now England's crown jewel, New York. As the ship approached the harbor, the landscape came into full view. To the left was the Hudson River and to the right, the East River. Windmills, church steeples, and tiled rooftops filled the skyline of the small settlement, a triangle of land one mile long and half a mile wide inhabited by Dutch, English, French, and Jewish settlers.[2] Dozens of ships filled the harbor and Sarah heard the clanging of ropes against tall wooden masts, the fluttering of sailcloth, and the shouting of orders from captains to their crew. Barrels, boxes, sacks, and chests were lowered into waiting boats and ferried to the long dock that jutted out like a strong burly arm. Men pushing carts and wheelbarrows over cobblestone streets hurried to the warehouses that lined the shoreline dropping off their collected goods. The sights, the sounds, and the smells—sweet fragrances of spices and oils, the salt spray, and the nose-turning stench of rotting fish and raw sewage from the free-roaming pigs,[3] were overwhelming.

Captain Bradley, a mariner and owner of transatlantic vessels,[4] told Sarah he'd heard that the ships that entered Manhattan's seaport carried valuable cargo—some worth more than fifty thousand pounds—from faraway places like the West Indies, Europe, and Madagascar.[5] His seafaring mates touted New York as the land of opportunity—a place where great riches could be had. Sarah knew trade was just one of the reasons her father brought their family to New York. They had lost their mother and the loss had been devastating. Now a single father, Captain Bradley wanted to leave the difficult past behind and make a fresh start. The New World held the promise of a better life for all of them.

Soon after arriving in Manhattan, Bradley met William Cox, a well-dressed, wealthy merchant who specialized in flour, the colony's most important trade good. A generous man with a paternal nature, he was an older bachelor in his midthirties. The two men quickly struck up a mutually beneficial relationship: Cox had money to invest in transatlantic voyages; Bradley had the connections to assist Cox in his business interests overseas. He also had a lovely daughter. Cox filed for a marriage license with Sarah Bradley in February 1685 and paid the governor a mandatory fee of half a guinea for his approval.[6] (The fee was a welcome addition to the governor's modest salary.) Two months later they were married in Manhattan on April 17, 1685.[7]

At fifteen, Sarah was a young bride, even for that time.[8] Most women in the seventeenth century married between the ages of twenty and twenty-two.[9] Cox was one of the richest men in the colony and Manhattan's most eligible bachelor; of all the available prospects he'd met while living in Manhattan for nearly a decade,[10] he chose Sarah. The rejected matrons must have wondered what was so special about the teenage newcomer. The clucking hens gossiped about the girl who disembarked carrying a suitcase that appeared too heavy for her size—a case which she carried close to her, protecting memories of her past. Cox knew right away when Captain Bradley introduced him to Sarah that she was the one. He wasted no time because he knew other suitors would quickly notice she was special and mature beyond her years.

Her maturity likely came from the loss of her mother. As the only female left in the Bradley family, she may have taken over her mother's household responsibilities. There is no mention of Sarah's mother, Mrs. Samuel Bradley, in the historical record and it is unclear for how long Sarah had been without her,[11] but Sarah learned from her mother's early modeling or a female caregiver the traditional English values that the husband was the "head of household," in charge of the public domain of business and politics, and the wife was the keeper of the private sphere of home and family. Sarah likely took care of her younger brothers, did the cooking, and managed the household while her father worked to support the family. As a mariner, he was often away and she carried the heavy burden on her small shoulders. She turned the tragic loss into a positive life lesson doing all that her mother would have wanted her to do and becoming, in all likelihood, like her, "lovely and accomplished."

Sarah brought to the marriage her most prized possessions. Her silver collection was substantial and included a tankard, cup, plate, sugar box and spoon, a saltcellar, porringers, tumbler, and two spoons. The total weight was 114 ounces, or about 7.125 pounds,[12] a very heavy dinner set. Silver was a sign of wealth and an investment in silver was only made when there was a surplus of funds.[13] Her collection may have belonged to her mother. It was so important to her she would do anything to keep it, including taking on the colonial authorities, as we will see.

She also brought her needlework. Almost all young girls in the seventeenth century were taught needlework, but hers shows that her parents valued education and they paid a tutor to teach her skills beyond the basic embroidery techniques. Her "chimneypiece,"[14] was a colorful framed embroidered picture of a theme or event meant to be hung above a fireplace as the room's decorative focal point. To create it, Sarah learned the fundamentals of arithmetic. She measured, counted, added and subtracted the stitches on her fabric. Sarah would have completed the chimneypiece after she completed at least one marking sampler. She would have undertaken a marking sampler when she was as young as five or six years old and learning basic embroidery stitches, the alphabet, and numbers. This early training was in preparation for her later adult responsibilities of sewing clothes and keeping track of her linens for her future family. Linens, such as handkerchiefs and napkins, were valuable household goods and she labeled hers by cross-stitching her initials and a number on one of the corners.[15]

Sarah also embroidered a coat of arms, a heraldic representation of her family name.[16] Not every young girl made a coat of arms but Sarah had an interest in her family history. With the help of her tutor she researched and read about the Bradleys from records kept at the College of Arms in London, an ancient institution founded in 1484.[17] With her nimble fingers and clever and inquisitive mind, she created needlework using an assortment of skills gleaned from her upper-class upbringing.

Sarah's wedding may have been held at the small Anglican church inside the fort, a star-shaped structure located at the southwest corner of Manhattan originally built as the headquarters of the Dutch West India Company to protect the colony against threatening outsiders.[18] But most weddings were performed by a justice of the peace at the bride's home.[19] Samuel Jr., Henry, Captain Bradley, and Cox's mother, Alice Bueno Cox (his only immediate family in Manhattan), would certainly have joined in the celebration eating and drinking traditional English wedding fare. Sarah served a wedding cake of dried fruits and spices and posset, a drink made of hot milk curdled with wine, ale, or other alcoholic liquor and flavored with nutmeg and cinnamon.[20] Captain Bradley had to have felt immensely proud. He found Sarah a good man. With his daughter's future secure and the Bradley family solidly established in polite New York society, his dream of a better life for all of them had come true, all within the first year of their arriving in the New World.

2

William Cox and the She-Merchant

Sarah moved into Sawkill Farm, Cox's country home north of the seaport in "Haarlem" (present day 74th Street and the East River). The 19¼-acre working farm named for the Sawkill Creek next to it is where Cox operated his milling operations. Legislation passed in 1678 called The Bolting Act gave New York an exclusive monopoly to mill and export flour.[1] It mandated that all grain for export from the New York area had to be ground, processed, and packaged in New York.[2] Governor Edmond Andros granted a flour-bolting concession to a handful of merchants that he knew and trusted to create a product of the highest quality. The economic future of the colony depended on it. Cox and his business partner, John Robinson, were among the chosen and they became exceptionally wealthy during the monopoly.[3] Cox became so wealthy he was able to purchase Sawkill Farm from Robinson in 1683, two years before he married Sarah, for £160, a large sum of money for the time.[4]

The purchase price of £160 reflects how quickly Manhattan real estate appreciated. Sawkill Farm was half of the

38¼–acre patent known as "The Riker and Lawrence Tract" near the present-day Roosevelt Island.[5] Robinson purchased the entire Riker and Lawrence Tract for "a quit rent of half a bushell of good winter wheate" in 1678.[6] And just fifty years earlier, in 1626, the director general of the Dutch West India Company, Peter Minuit, purchased the entire 22,000-acre island of Manhattan from the Indigenous people there for 60 guilders or $24 (about $1,143 in 2020 dollars).[7]

Sarah quickly learned real estate was her future; it was a currency that separated the haves from the have-nots. Land, more than money, was a symbol of wealth and social status in the new emerging colonial economy.

Sawkill Farm had a grist mill, a main house, several single tenements for the enslaved workers, a buttery, vegetable and herb gardens, acres of pastures for the horses, and plenty of woods. The surrounding areas were wilderness and farmland and this area was in the Out Ward, one of the six wards that divided up Manhattan. The Out Ward got its name for being outside the city and Cox knew the area well as its alderman on the city council.[8]

The farm was a cool place to escape the summer heat, but if Sarah wanted to return to the city, she could use one of Cox's two horses and ride on rutted trails for fourteen to fifteen miles. Or she could take a local boat called a sloop—a sailboat with a single mast that typically has one headsail in front of the mast and one mainsail behind the mast—for a two- to three-hour ride down the East River to the harbor where she first glimpsed her New World.

The production of flour was *the* activity of the farm and Cox's enslaved man, Titus, worked alongside him.[9] Cox purchased large quantities of grain when it was in season from dealers and local farmers and processed it into white flour, grinding it to an exact standard of fineness. The flour was then sifted and packed in wooden casks held together with a dozen hoops that tightly sealed the casks to preserve the flour's freshness. The heads of the barrels were stamped with a fire-hot branding iron to identify the contents. "SF 196" meant "superfine" white flour and the "196" was the weight in pounds that the barrel contained. By law, the barrels were required to weigh 196 pounds. Cox and Titus made sure the casks were packed full and level, measuring, adding, and subtracting the contents until they were just right. Then the casks were carefully transported to the seaport in a wagon pulled by one of Cox's horses and loaded onto ships bound for the West Indies where the flour was used to make bread to feed the enslaved workers and the plantation owners.

While Cox supervised operations at the grist mill, Sarah did housewifery on their country estate. Typical chores included tending the vegetable and herb gardens, growing beets, carrots, culinary and medicinal herbs, onions, and peas;[10] cooking, preserving fruits and vegetables, making soap and candles, spinning flax, dyeing yarn, weaving cloth, sewing clothes, and working in the buttery making cheese and butter.[11] One of the enslaved servants, Moll, helped Sarah with the washing, food preparation, and any additional chores. It was a simple life and Sarah dressed accordingly in a casual work dress made of cotton and pinned her hair up to keep it out of her face.

For well over a year, Sarah watched the long arms of the grist mill churn. She heard the grinding of wheat and corn and she smelled the fire stoked for the branding iron. She was seventeen years old, without children, and she was restless. A keen observer of Cox's business operations she noted that it involved measuring, counting, adding, and subtracting like her needlework. A simplified version of a complex business, of course, but it gave her an idea.

She had met the wives of Cox's merchant friends and knew that some worked with their husbands as shopkeepers and operators of small businesses. The roles of women were starting to change and they balanced their traditional roles with careers as she-merchants. Frederick Philipse's wife, Margaret Hardenbroeck, was especially inspiring. She inherited a fleet of ships from her first husband and operated a successful business importing dry goods from London. In the hold of her fluyts—Dutch sailing vessels with a capacious storage area for cargo—she brought back to the city women's and girls' bodices, knives, sword blades, frying pans, chimney bricks, bridle bits for horse harnesses, and pewter toys for children, to name a few.[12] Sarah noticed there was an especially strong desire among wealthy New Yorkers for fine clothes like those worn by the British landed gentry and nobility. She had learned all about upper-class fashion and style from her mother; Cox knew about business and foreign trade. Together they could open a retail shop of imported high-end goods in the city where men and women came to do their shopping. English law restricted married women in the labor market, however. Under the laws of coverture a married woman was *feme covert*, a French term meaning that she was "covered" by her husband; she was his property and she did not have a legal identity of her own. She could not buy or sell property or goods, incur debts, or sign contracts.[13] Cox would need to finance the operation and take on all the legal liabilities. The idea excited Cox; it would diversify his financial portfolio and give Sarah a productive and creative outlet. A win–win situation.

On January 21, 1687, a year and a half after their wedding, Cox purchased another property from John Robinson, a splendid mansion in the city located at 119–121 Pearl Street near the present-day Hanover Square.[14] Many merchants operated shops out of their homes on Pearl Street because it was near the wharf and along the East River where ships could easily load and unload goods.[15]

Manhattan was a city of more than seven hundred houses closely built on short blocks that filled the compact area of just two and a half square miles. A wall protected the city with gates on the east and west sides. Pearl Street was centrally located within the city wall, just steps from the east gate and marked the original eastern shoreline of the lower part of Manhattan. It was named for the plentiful supply of large oysters the size of a dinner plate in the East River where they were harvested in the months with a letter *r* in the name—September, October, November, December, January, February, March, and April.[16]

Sarah's new home was of the Dutch style dating back to the colony's early years when the Dutch West India Company operated a trading post trading furs with the Indigenous nations. Built for Govert Loockermans, a wealthy Dutch fur trader and ship owner who began his career in the colony in 1633 as an assistant cook on a ship, his mansion was one of the finest homes in the colony.[17] It had the traditional high stoop and gabled ends that were notched like steps. The roof was sheathed with red and black tiles like many of the homes in Holland and the sizeable property was about thirty-eight feet in front by forty-eight feet in depth, with a kitchen extension of twenty square feet, likely used as the quarters for Titus and Moll. Along the eastern side of the building ran a cartway, now forming a part of what is known as Hanover Street, and nearly one hundred feet in the rear of the house, on the back lane called "the sloot," or ditch, stood a stable or coach house some twenty by forty feet.[18] A portion of the house may have been used as a warehouse to keep the surplus inventory. The mansion faced the harbor, and even then waterfront property was a sign of wealth and status. A wide road ran parallel to the waterfront and to protect the riverbank from erosion, Loockermans installed a sturdy wall made of stacked wooden planks. The street later became known as Wall Street and today is associated with the Financial District.

Cox invested heavily in dry goods from the great London firms and filled their sizeable shop with cloth, ribbons, buttons, thread, clothing, seed and agricultural implements, glassware, earthenware, and a number of household items including nails.[19] They also sold Cox's wheat flour from Sawkill Farm and goods from the surrounding area: Rhode Island cheese and barreled pork, Long Island whale oil, fruit, and parcels of woolen cloth.[20] Sarah picked out the women's and children's clothing—the gloves, shoes, hose, and hats—and all of the sewing notions and textiles of all colors and kinds. Her taste was exquisite, the fabrics were rich, colorful, and plush.

A popular way for London wholesalers to display the latest fashions was through "fashion babies," dolls dressed in apparel from London milliners' textiles.[21] Sarah received a fashion baby in "milliners' boxes" and selected the clothes from the doll's wardrobe.[22] (After the fashion season, the fashion babies were recycled as dolls for lucky privileged little girls.)[23] Among the women's favorites were mantuas—long gowns made from brightly colored silk and satin. The shop carried finished mantuas as well as fabrics to have them made by local seamstresses—usually enslaved women. The latest women's styles showed delicate handmade lace on the eye-catchingly low neckline and matching brocade shoes.[24] Sarah had seen these on the ladies in England; her mother likely dressed in the flowing gowns. She knew firsthand that getting dressed was a multistep process that required an extra pair of hands to fasten the corset and help with the many slips and petticoats that produced the regal-looking dress fitted at the bodice with a full skirt.[25] Moll would have helped her by buttoning, fastening, and hooking.

Sarah learned retail by being a customer herself. She watched, listened, and learned how the other she-merchants helped their customers pick out their goods and manage the sales transactions. Many of the purchases were bought on credit. By extending credit, Cox created a web of loyalty from cash-strapped customers who felt the effects of the Navigation Acts. The law required that all goods imported into the colony first go by way of England, which added enormously to the cost of transport and depressed the market for North American goods abroad. The result was a crippling shortage of cash. Without gold and silver coins called *specie*, the colonists could not purchase things outright. Cox accepted other currencies like Dutch money that still circulated from when the Dutch ruled the colony decades before and Indigenous wampum, small purple and white cylindrical beads made from clam and whelk shells found along the shores of Narragansett Bay and Long Island Sound.[26]

People from as far away as Boston came to shop in the Coxes' store. Ladies like Remembrance Lippingcott, Sarah Catchum, Abigail Emry, Marcy Pettit, Marcey Pillman, and Rebecca Hubbard had heard about the young proprietress of Pearl Street and established accounts.[27] And so did some of the most prominent members of the community—William Merritt, the current mayor of New York City; Dr. Lockhart, one of the few doctors in the colony; and Colonel Abraham de Peyster, a wealthy merchant and politician who remarked Sarah was "lovely and accomplished."[28]

Cox had to have been immensely proud of his talented wife and Sarah was delighted that Cox supported her ambitious undertaking. She maintained her duties of housewifery between business hours and bedtime and Cox commuted back and forth by horseback to Sawkill Farm to oversee the flour operation. A bride at fifteen, a she-merchant at seventeen, Sarah was a trailblazer for her time. But this energizing life as a she-merchant would soon be interrupted.

3

Mayhem and Tragedy

In 1688 King James II ordered that the Province of New York be included with the Dominion of New England to consolidate the administration of the New England colonies into a supercolony made up of all of New England plus New York, New Jersey, and Pennsylvania.[1] Edmond Andros had been made the governor of the new Dominion of New England in addition to New York. In an official ceremony in Manhattan to show that New York was no longer a separate entity with its own administration, Andros broke the New York Provincial Seal in half. He then hoisted the flag of New England over the fort, seized all the provincial records, and returned to Boston leaving Colonel Francis Nicholson behind as lieutenant governor.[2] Soon it was learned that in addition to the reorganization of the New England colonies, there was an upheaval in the monarchy. The Catholic James II was forced from the throne in a "Glorious Revolution" that saw William of Orange and his wife, Mary, James's eldest daughter, installed as joint Protestant monarchs.

A courier dispatched on a ship from London delivered

word of the new monarchs to Boston, the capital of the Dominion. The news caused an uprising and Bostonians overthrew their government. Andros had been good to Cox giving him a special concession for bolting flour, but he had made a lot of enemies over the years and he was a very unpopular governor. He and some of his equally unpopular officials who had been loyal to King James were arrested. Andros attempted to flee Boston dressed in women's clothing but, unfamiliar with the nuances of women's attire, gave away his disguise when his boots showed under the dress.[3] An angry mob threw him and others in jail and he was later sent to England in chains.[4]

New York citizens feared an attack on the city by groups loyal to James II called Jacobites. In an effort to thwart the attack, on May 31, 1689, the local New York City militia declared their allegiance to the new monarch by seizing the fort. Jacob Leisler, a wealthy merchant from Frankfurt, Germany, with a wife and seven children, took a leadership role in the uprising and proclaimed himself lieutenant governor and commander in chief of the Province of New York. Among his followers who joined the militia were the shopkeepers, craftsmen, sailors, cart men, and laborers who formed the bulk of the city's population.[5] Leisler moved into the governor's residence in the fort and set up his camp.

The local militia set up a Committee of Safety to govern New York City until the colony resumed its normal operations with a new governor appointed by the monarchs, William and Mary. Cox was a strong supporter of Jacob Leisler; they had served as jurors in an Admiralty Court case that involved large quantities of stolen French brandy.[6] Leisler asked

Cox to serve on the Committee of Safety, a prestigious position of some importance and responsibility reserved only for leading citizens. Sarah learned through Cox's insider status the up-to-the-minute details as Leisler and his militia resisted forces that supported James II. There was mayhem in the streets: anti-Leislerians threatened and ambushed people, ransacked homes and stores, intercepted mail, and arrested people for questioning. Sarah's store was safe, no doubt, because of Cox's politics, but the New York described by Virginia planter William Byrd in 1685 as "a pretty pleasant towne"[7] had become a colony under siege wracked with violence and rebellion. Sarah had to have been terrified and maybe she questioned her decision to move to the city. The Out Ward in the wilderness, away from the violence, may have seemed a safer place to be. But Cox was needed in the city and Sarah stayed with him to keep the shop open and protect their home.

On April 9, 1689, about two years after buying the Pearl Street house, Cox bought a house from Lucas Teinhoven and his wife located on the north side of Wall Street, a street that was undergoing a sort of urban renewal with the development of a nicer class of homes than had been in that part of the city.[8] Sarah and Cox moved into 56 Wall Street, just two blocks north of their Pearl Street shop, and furnished it opulently. They were extraordinarily wealthy now, in large part from the success of the shop.

The turmoil in the city may have awakened in Cox the need to protect all that he owned and loved. He was nearly forty years old and he had not, until now, thought to preserve his legacy. From the desk in his new home, Cox put quill pen to parchment and wrote his Last Will and Testament, a detailed and thoughtful document that reflected his level of wealth, his network of intimates, and his primary concerns in life. Dated July 15, 1689, his will ensured that his assets would be properly dispersed and that his enslaved workers kept in the family. His intentions were specific and generous to his "dear and loving wife," Sarah, her two brothers, Samuel Jr. and Henry (minors at the time), his mother, housekeeper Dorothy Lee, servant Jacob Mayle, and his friend Richard Jones.

Cox owned six properties in New York and he bequeathed half of them to Sarah and the other half to Samuel Jr. He allowed Sarah to have first pick of the house she wanted to live in—Pearl Street or Wall Street—and Samuel Jr. was to take the other. At the end of the will, however, Cox made a clarification based on a conversation he'd had with his mother. He wanted Samuel Jr. to have the Wall Street house because he made a promise to his mother that there would be no arguing about who should get the home he was currently living in. Sarah and Cox did not have any children, and it appears he did not expect to have any because he gave Samuel Jr. a directive to carry on the Cox name. He wrote that if Samuel Jr. ever had a son, "he shall call his name Cox Bradley and his children after him the same name."[9] Cox not only wanted his name to continue, he provided a place for that son to live at 56 Wall Street.

To Sarah's other brother, Henry, he gave Sawkill Farm, £100 for when he came of age, and a quarter of a ship he owned, the *James*, with all the profits that went with it. Cox must have been quite fond of Henry because he set him up with both cash and a career in bolting and exporting flour as well as a vessel to transport it. He left £500 to his mother and £10 to Dorothy Lee.

Cox probably did not discuss the terms of his will with Sarah. He seemed to have written it hastily, changing his mind at the end after he discussed the final financial details with his mother. Cox giving the newer, finer, more opulently furnished home to Samuel Jr. instead of Sarah is an interesting and disturbing turn of events. He clearly thought a young man with a future to carry on the mandated Cox name should have a nicer home than his wife. Was he disappointed with Sarah for not having borne him a child and he was, in effect, punishing her? It seems so. He was a businessman not a physician and he clearly did not understand that he carried half of the responsibility for producing a child. This is the second time a man determined Sarah's future. The first was her father arranging her marriage to Cox. If Sarah wanted the Wall Street house, she would have to wait and sort it out with her brother later.

Jacob Leisler asked Cox to go to eastern New Jersey to inform the residents that William and Mary had ascended the throne. There were no newspapers in New York City at the time; it would be another twenty-one years before information was disseminated in printed form. News had to be delivered in person, especially news of such magnitude as a new monarchy. The event was a ceremonial occasion requiring full fashion regalia. Cox's access to the best fashion houses in London and a fashion-forward wife guaranteed he would be a handsome showpiece in his finest long curly wig, knee-length brocade coat, embroidered waistcoat with a lace cravat, breeches, stockings, and silver buckled shoes.[10]

In August 1689, just three weeks after Cox wrote his will, Cox left Sarah in Manhattan. He boarded his sloop and set sail for Staten Island for what was to be a one-day trip. He left his vessel at a point and went the rest of the way by canoe. After reading the king's Proclamation to a large crowd of anxious and excited citizens and a brief visit with the authorities of the town, he returned to the sloop again by canoe. He paddled alongside the sloop. A sudden strong gust of wind caused him to lose his balance. He was able to stand up and he reached for the sloop's rail, but he lost his balance again and fell into the water. Onlookers heard the splash and saw his clumsy fall. They laughed at the regal middle-aged man awkwardly flailing to right himself. Cox's shoes touched the bottom and everyone believed he was safe and well: his chin was above water and his brocade coat could be seen inches beneath the waves. Soon however, Cox's coat disappeared beneath the surface. He was sinking into the cold, dark mud. It was like the open mouth of a serpent was sucking him in. The more he struggled to free himself, the deeper down he went. His water-soaked finery acted like ballast in a sinking ship. Cox strained to reach for the canoe, but it was too far. Every inch was too far. A witness reported that "striving to get out, bobbing his head under, [he] received too much water in. They brought him ashore with life in him but all would not fetch him againe."[11] This was before the days of CPR (cardiopulmonary resuscitation), and witnesses were unable to resuscitate him.

The detailed account of Cox's accident and drowning at Captain Cornelius Point in Staten Island was reported by John Tuder, a political enemy of Cox. He claimed in a letter to the ousted lieutenant governor, Francis Nicholson, that Cox's trip was a vanity play "to show his fine clothes." The vitriol didn't stop there. Of Sarah, he flippantly said, "There is a good rich widow left."[12]

There is no record of who conveyed the tragic news to Sarah or her reaction when his body was returned to her. We can only image her shock. One minute she was enjoying a secure and comfortable life with her husband of four years, the next minute she was a nineteen-year-old widow with an uncertain future. It was a time when a comforting mother was desperately needed. This was her second big loss: first her mother, and now her husband. It is possible that her mother-in-law was supportive, but Alice Cox had just lost her only son and she had her own pain to deal with. From Cox's discussion with his mother over his will it appeared they had an intimate mother-son relationship. Sarah's next-door neighbor, Elsie, stepdaughter of Govert Loockermans, and wife of Jacob Leisler, had been a young widow before she married Leisler. She may have knocked on Sarah's door offering comforting sympathy. Sarah's father and brothers lived in the area and they certainly would have come immediately upon hearing the devastating news. They would have searched for her either at the shop on Pearl Street or the Wall Street home.

Jacob Leisler approved what was the equivalent of a state funeral for Cox. A man of Cox's stature merited such an elaborate funeral, especially since he died in the service of the

Crown. One witness reported that the whole town turned out to attend the service. Among the choice of funeral gifts typically given to mourners—gloves, silver spoons, bottles of wine, scarfs, handkerchiefs, or a ring with the deceased's initials—Sarah gave a pair of white gloves to every man and woman to wear during the funeral.[13] In keeping with tradition, Sarah would have worn a long black mourning gown.

Cox was laid in state in the fort with British flags flown at half-mast all over the city including on the ships in the harbor. The long funeral procession, accompanied by the slow mournful beat of drums, ran from the fort north to Broadway, the widest street in the city. Sarah could look to the west of Broadway and see orchards, gardens, and a few homes overlooking the Hudson River.[14] To the east she would have seen where she and most of the residents lived. As the cortege moved beyond the west gate in the wall to the churchyard, guns fired until Cox was buried. Afterward, the community ate, drank, and smoked. There were the traditional small funeral cakes made with caraway seeds, a pipe of wine and rum, and tapers to light the clay pipes.[15] For the porters and dock workers, there was a barrel of beer.[16]

Cox's will was proved in the Court of Sessions on August 9, 1689, three weeks after he wrote it. As was the custom, a letter of administration was filed asking that an inventory be made of Cox's estate by his executors, Jacob Mayle, a Jamaican man who managed Cox's accounts, and Richard Jones, a Quaker merchant in Manhattan. The petition was filed by John Oort, an associate of Cox's. Oort complained that the executors asked him for a £5000 bond (which he couldn't pay) before conducting the inventory. Leisler stepped in and ordered that the inventory be made. Cox's inventory is a window into the economy in New York City in 1689 and it shows his vast network. It also offers a glimpse into the world in which Sarah and Cox lived. Together they had a partnership of success and good taste.

Cox was a man of significant means with an estate valued at £1900—a very substantial sum compared to the country traders who walked the streets selling parcels of timber and containers of foodstuffs like pickled oysters to raise any amount of cash.[17] The inventory taken on September 11, 1689, listed every item he owned including the items in the shop. It was written on seven long narrow pages with a very sharp quill pen. The work of accounting for every needle and thread, button and bobbin was a time-consuming task that shed light on the historical significance of material goods in the late seventeenth century. Every item mattered because it took so much effort to either make it or import it.

Of all the rooms in Cox's six properties, it is fortuitous that the only room specifically identified and inventoried was Sarah's bedroom in 56 Wall Street. From the number of furnishings listed in "The Chamber of the Widow Cox," the room was large and beautifully appointed. A goose feather bed was adorned with bolsters, pillows, sheets, blankets, and a quilt. She drew curtains with gold fringe and used two chests of drawers for storage. On one of the chests she kept a dressing box and glass case, on the other a mirror called a looking glass that she probably used to dress by. In the reflection of the sterling silver mirror, Sarah could see herself surrounded by the finest of the finest. She had arranged twelve turkey work chairs throughout the bedroom. A turkey work

covering on a chair was a form of knotted embroidery produced by professional weavers in England who used worsted
wool closely shorn to imitate the colorful geometrically styl-
ized flowers found in Turkish carpets.[18] Somewhere in her
bedroom, perhaps in the drawer of one of her chests, Sarah
kept her prized collection of silver.[19]

Sarah informed Jacob Mayle that the silver collection was
not part of Cox's estate, it was exempt from the inventory
because it was hers before the marriage when she was a single
woman and had *feme sole* status under the law of coverture.
Single women, or *feme sole*, did have full economic identities and control of their property, unlike married women,
feme covert, who did not.[20] Sarah's statement to Jacob Mayle
makes clear she understood that she gave up her individual
rights when marrying Cox. Her father decided that her marriage to Cox was far better than remaining single. Wealth
and status with Cox versus matronhood with benefits was
an easy decision to make. Sarah would agree it was a sacri-
fice worth making.

In addition to the hundreds of items in the shop, the inventory lists 548 gallons of rum, 756 bushels of salt, 37 gallons of wine, large quantities of textiles, a pair of garnets, 18
old books, 2 enslaved people—Titus (£30) and Moll (£25),
2 horses—one gray and the other bay (£11), pistols, holsters
and sword, a saddle, and barrels and barrels of flour.

All of Cox's debtors are listed by name and the 150 debts
owed to him totaled about £500. Even Captain Bradley
borrowed £7. Cox kept £239 in cash on hand. Most of the
colonists in Manhattan, or anywhere in the North American colonies, did not possess that much money. The large

amount of ready cash shows the fluidity of his finances and the robustness of his commerce. Cox kept £14 ready money for Captain Bradley suggesting that he acted as Bradley's personal bank.

Jacob Mayle recorded in detail Cox's interest in more than half a dozen transatlantic voyages. He noted the destination of the voyages, how much Cox invested, and to whom he consigned the money.[21] As the daughter of a transatlantic ship owner, Sarah would have heard about the faraway places of Jamaica, Barbados, and the Dutch islands of Suriname and Curassow. She may have even visited them at a very early age.

Cox spent £12 for a voyage to Madagascar, the fourth largest island in the world off the coast of Africa. Several New York merchants purchased enslaved Africans there and sold them in New York along the wharves on the waterfront and out of taverns at premium prices.[22] Slavery was not new to New York: it was part of the colony's history from when it was a Dutch settlement.[23] Young able-bodied men and women were preferred and attracted the highest prices at auction. They were thought to have the longest "shelf life" and they were more likely to survive the Middle Passage, those hellish months crossing the Atlantic where the captives were often confined and left to stew in their own excrement as the ship pitched and rolled. Some ship captains stuffed the hold of their ship with as much human cargo as they could fit to keep their numbers and profit margin high. Many of those enslaved died a horrible death during transport on the vessels of oppression. Cox owned two people who were enslaved. More than likely they were from Madagascar and the £12 investment was to help defray the cost of the voyage. Merchants who could afford ventures to Madagascar or West Africa did so to buy people to enslave for their personal use.[24] Sarah would have known how Cox acquired Moll and Titus, the only ones Sarah was aware Cox owned. She saw men offloading human cargo from the ships in the harbor. Owning enslaved people was a sign of wealth, and the free labor helped Cox run his profitable flour business as well as maintain his properties. The extra pair of hands assisted Sarah with the burden of the household chores and allowed her to pursue her own interests as a she-merchant. Cox and Sarah amassed wealth and enjoyed a luxurious lifestyle because of their free enslaved labor.

The inventory suggests that while Leisler granted Cox a grand funeral, his gratitude for Cox's service was short-lived. Leisler's men confiscated timber and boards worth over £11 from Cox's property and he tied up Cox's estate in bureaucratic red tape, making it impossible for Sarah to receive her inheritance. She was permitted to live in Cox's home on Pearl Street with Titus, Moll, and Dorothy Lee, but she could not have the money, goods in the shop, or other properties. Sarah's brothers were minors and her father, for some unknown reason, was unable to help her fight the matter in court. With no legal rights to defend herself, Sarah's hands were tied. She shuttered the store and waited until the political situation turned in her favor.

4

Debts and Bills

Sarah was wealthy in theory but cash poor. She understood that a woman's place in colonial society was through her husband. With Cox gone she was cast adrift. Sarah did what many women did to survive: sometime in 1690, a year after Cox's death, she married John Oort, a Dutch merchant and former ship captain who had been involved in the administration of Cox's estate. It is doubtful that Sarah's father had as much to do with her marrying Oort as he did with Cox. Sarah was about twenty years old and she had the experience of four years of marriage and a year of grieving behind her. She could make up her own mind. It was about this time that Samuel Jr. was involved in a land transaction for 56 Wall Street.[1] Sarah was with him when he sold Cox's former house to a Scottish sea captain named Captain William Kidd who lived in New York when he wasn't on privateering assignments.

In March 1691 things began to change politically for the better. The new legitimate governor sent by the king, Henry

Sloughter, arrived in New York. Captain Kidd also returned to New York from a privateering voyage in the West Indies. As a privateer, Kidd was hired to legally plunder and seize enemy French ships. During wartime, the resources of warring countries were stretched to the limit and privateers, "private men of war," were extra hired hands who owned their own armed vessel and served as an auxiliary to England's navy. Kidd's privateer assignment was detailed on a document called a "letter of marque and reprisal." It was a license to raid enemy ships and take prizes. The prizes—captured enemy ships and their cargo—were delivered to the British Admiralty Court where the value of the take was assessed and a percentage given to the investors. Kidd was essentially given permission to act as a pirate, but since he had legal authorization in a letter of marque, he was considered a privateer.

England's conflict with France over the supremacy of North America called King William's War had begun in 1688 and was still ongoing. Kidd had been hired as a privateer by Christopher Codrington, governor of the Leeward Islands, an English colony in the West Indies, to help ward off the French. Kidd saw action on the tiny French island of Marie Galante (near Guadeloupe) and was sent to help at the island of St. Martin but his men preferred piracy to legal plundering and stole his twenty-gun vessel, the *Blessed William*, while he was on shore at St. Martin.[2] The men scrambled to hide and disperse in the one place that was safe for pirates—New York City. They took with them, carefully stashed among their own loot, Kidd's share of the booty worth £2000.[3] Kidd's successful mission for the governor earned him high praise and as a thank-you gift, Codrington replaced the *Blessed William* with a captured French ship that Kidd named the *Antigua*.[4] The *Antigua* was a brigantine, a two-masted sailing vessel with a square-rigged foremast and a fore-and-aft-rigged mainmast.[5] Kidd was determined to get his money back from his mutinous crew and over the winter of 1690–1691 the chase in his new ship brought him to New York.[6]

Kidd's return to New York could not have been timelier. He quickly assessed the chaotic political situation and seized the opportunity to assist Governor Sloughter in quelling Leisler's stronghold on the colony. The decision was an easy one for Kidd; there was no love lost between the two men. In a Dutch document dated March 16, 1691, Leisler referred to Kidd as a "blasphemous privateer."[7] Kidd volunteered his much-needed ship to carry arms to the west side of the island where Leisler was hunkered down in the fort. With guns pointed at the barracks and at the acting governor's house, Leisler quickly understood that the fight was over. When he surrendered, the period known as Leisler's Rebellion had finally ended.

The local assembly granted Kidd a generous reward of £150 for helping to restore order to the colony. He also won the hearts of many anti-Leislerians who had endured the political strife that tore at their livelihoods and personal security. Kidd was the man of the hour. The community called him a war hero and he was considered a highly respected member of polite New York society. Well-dressed and well-built with a hint of a Scottish accent, Captain Kidd was a memorable and attractive figure in the colony at the time.

Joyous celebrations broke out throughout the colony from

thankful citizens relieved that stability had finally been restored and that justice would be forthcoming to Leisler and
his accomplice, son-in-law Jacob Milborne, eight years his
junior and recently married to his daughter, Mary. Leisler
and Milborne were arrested, accused of treason, and tried
by a specially commissioned court that condemned both of
them to death.[8]

Sarah may have been relieved the Leisler nightmare was
over, but heavyhearted over her own distressing circumstances. Oort had been unable to help her in her legal fight
against Leisler's administration to regain her inheritance,
and he was unable to sustain his livelihood as a merchant
during Leisler's reign. He joined other merchants in a letter
to King William pleading for financial relief.[9] In order to
pay his bills, Oort borrowed money from several wealthy
merchants and three widows.[10] The money Oort borrowed
from the widows—£6 each—was not insignificant. The av-
erage loan William Cox made to his customers was £3.3s
(three pounds, three shillings), or about half of what Oort
received from three different women. Oort must have had
some qualities Sarah admired or she would not have married
him, but Sarah entered into the marriage, as many women
did, for financial security and legal protection. Love came
second. Oort's instability and indebtedness deteriorated her
loveless one-year marriage. When Sarah learned of Oort's
indebtedness to three—probably lonely—widows, she may
have become suspicious and wondered what convincing line
Oort used on them. He must have charmed them like he
charmed her with his Dutch accent. There is no record of
Oort owning property in Manhattan so it is very likely that

he lived in Sarah's Pearl Street house among her fine furnishings. In a dark moment, she may have thought he had the telltale signs of a gold digger. No matter how much Sarah may have wished things were different, however, under the law of coverture she was powerless to change her situation. She was a minor in the eyes of the law.[11] Divorce was not an option—the courts rarely granted divorces to women in the colonial period. The rights of the husband were almost always absolute.[12] Only the death of the husband terminated the restrictions imposed on the *feme covert*.

It was sometime during the festivities celebrating the end of Leisler's rule that Sarah had crossed paths with Captain Kidd. It had been two years since they met over the purchase of Cox's Wall Street house. Sarah remembered Kidd well, he had a physical presence that exuded confidence; he was well-spoken and his signature on the deed was handsome and practiced—*"Wm. Kidd."* He had acquired a "competent estate" of properties and had signed his name on many deeds, according to land records.[13] Curiously enough, one of the properties he owned was near Sarah at 86-90 Pearl Street. Among his other properties was a fine house and seventy-five feet of ground on Tienhoven Street—now known as 25, 27, and 29 Pine Street; another lot on the north side of Pearl Street 150 feet west of Old Slip; and 52-56 Water Street between Old Slip and Coenties Slips.[14] Kidd was wealthy, stable, and his rugged good looks impressed Sarah—a lot.

Kidd undoubtedly took notice of Sarah at their first meeting but he had no time for romance; he was a mariner through and through. He had accepted a privateering assignment with Governor Codrington to fight the French in the West Indies and he would be gone for an indefinite period of time. Sarah could not wait for him, even if she wanted to; she needed and wanted someone to help her restabilize after Cox's sudden and tragic death. Oort had been available and very interested.

Sarah and Kidd likely became reacquainted at one of the many taverns by the water, near where she lived. With the expansion of trade, more people had come to the city. In a period of twenty-five years, from 1694 to 1720, more than fifty new taverns opened.[15] With names like the Black Horse Tavern and Old King's Arms, taverns, also called public houses, ordinaries, or inns, were popular meeting places for residents and travelers. Many offered overnight accommodations for people and horses; all were lively places for food, drink, entertainment, and the passing of secrets. Kidd would have had a favorite hangout; he was known to like his liquor and engage in boisterous conversation when he had had a few tankards too many.[16] Sarah and Kidd may have had one of the popular drinks of flip or punch. (Flip was made in pitchers of two-thirds strong beer and rum. A red-hot iron loggerhead made it foam and gave it a unique burnt taste. Punch was the combination of tea, rum, arrack, sugar, lemons, and water in a large bowl, mixed and ladled into a tankard.)[17] Sarah was still married to Oort and the time they spent together was an innocent get-reacquainted chat. Kidd knew Oort well— he had been one of Kidd's officers a few years back.[18] How many times Sarah and Kidd met is unclear but the evidence suggests that their relationship changed from a business acquaintance to a warm and trusting friendship in a very short period of time. In the din of the noisy tavern, it is nearly certain she shared the details of Oort's financial failures and her deeply felt humiliation and shame. Her youthful expression gave way to the fact she was at wit's end. Kidd listened in the way a mariner listened for the change in the wind, the crashing of waves, and the desperate caw of seabirds sounding the alarm that a storm was approaching. Sarah saw the intent look in his dark brown eyes framed by his shoulder-length wig.[19] It was the look of a man who understood the problem but did not hint to the solution.

The next time they met, John Oort was dead. There were no details of the death in the public record but many believed it was sudden and unexpected.

5

Dead Men Tell No Tales

The municipal document granted on short notice by the governor for a premium fee of £500 was brief and to the point:[1] *A license of marriage granted unto Captain William Kidd of New York, Gentleman, of the one part, and Sarah Oort, the widow of John Oort, late of New York, merchant, deceased, May 16, 1691.*[2]

It was a rainy Wednesday in Manhattan on the day of their wedding, just two days after Oort's death. Sarah was a twice-widowed twenty-one-year-old and Kidd was thirty-seven. Jacob Leisler and Jacob Milborne were hanged in the public square in what is now City Hall Park.[3] Sarah and Kidd attended the early morning hanging before their wedding. Kidd and a fellow Scot named Colonel Robert Livingston stood so close to the scaffolding they saw the rain drizzling down the face of Jacob Milborne and heard his last words: "We are thoroughly wet with rain, but in a little time we shall be washed with the Holy Spirit."[4] As the handkerchief was tied around Jacob Leisler's head he cried out, "I hope my eyes shall see our Lord Jesus Christ in heaven; I am ready! I am ready!"[5]

Sarah and Kidd's love match happened fast in a turbulent time. The fear and uncertainty may have focused Sarah on the brevity of life. It had been seven years since she arrived in New York, and she had learned a lot about men and marriage: her first was arranged, her second was for convenience, this one was for love. Sarah knew that the timing of her marriage so soon after Oort's death was suspicious, that some might wonder if Kidd had something to do with the Dutch merchant's sudden demise. Did he kill him or have him killed so he could marry Sarah? Or, did Sarah, with the help of an accomplice, organize the fatal event so she could marry the man she loved?

Sarah had made short work of the procedures and protocols of Oort's death. He died intestate (without leaving a will), so Sarah filed for the letter of administration, initiated an inventory of his meager estate, contacted the coroner, and held a funeral all within twenty-four hours of his death.[6] The funeral expense of £30 was added to the list of debts Oort owed to the merchants and the three widows.[7] It all went so smoothly she may have seen it as a meant-to-be sign that she was supposed to have a promising new future.

Sarah knew her behavior was unconventional but it didn't dissuade her from going through with the sudden nuptials. The couple's bold news shook the community known for its love of gossip. She was willing to tolerate the loud whispers about the widow and the war hero in taverns, street corners, and behind closed doors—it gave people something to talk about. She may have humorously thought their marriage was a public service of sorts.

Sarah and Kidd were such solid citizens and highly respected members of New York society that an investigation into Oort's death was not initiated and no untoward behavior was ever proven. Sarah may have disregarded the social norm of grieving a year for her husband before remarrying, but what the community would come to understand was that she knew a great opportunity when it came her way. Sarah was taken with Kidd, and he with her. Nothing seemed to faze her. This was a new beginning and she was open to all that it might bring.

They set up Sarah's Pearl Street home and a list of the goods and chattels made at the time showed they lived surrounded by luxurious furnishings.[8] The large collection of pewter plates and drinking glasses suggests that the Kidds hosted large, lavish dinner parties. The meals were cooked with a skillet and two iron pots, and meat was lifted out of the pot with a flesh fork, unusual for the time. They set the table with two pewter saltcellars (small footed bowls) and Sarah had a choice of tablecloths and napkins. (People primarily ate their food with their hands so numerous napkins were a luxury item.) Barrels of cider were available for everyone to enjoy in pewter tankards.

Dorothy Lee, Sarah's longtime housekeeper, likely shook out their six rugs including the only turkey work carpet in Manhattan, crisped the linen sheets with smoothing irons, and made up the four-poster feather beds with valences and curtains.[9] On cold nights, Lee likely filled the warming pan with hot coals and put it between the sheets among the bolsters and pillows. In the morning, she may have wound the clock that ordered their days, emptied two bed pans, and polished four looking glasses for Sarah and Kidd to dress by. They kept fires going in the two fireplaces, carefully implementing the fire tongs to make sure the ashes did not blow past the decorative fenders. They used candles to keep the house well lit, trimming their wicks in the brass, pewter, and tin candlesticks.

While Sarah minded things at Pearl Street, Kidd worked as a merchant sea captain delivering goods to and from the Caribbean. His route took him south where he touched base in Antigua, then headed north, sometimes stopping in Boston.[10] The West Indies needed food, wood to build things, and an assortment of manufactured goods.[11] Flour, pine, and white oak were readily available in New York. In turn, the West Indies was an abundant source of sugar, rum, and spices for the northern colonies. Sailing in the *Antigua*, Kidd shuttled cargo back and forth taking on privateering jobs when he was needed.

A year into their marriage, Sarah received a written notice from the acting governor, Richard Ingoldsby, informing her that as the administratrix of the estate of John Oort she had neglected to exhibit the inventory of Oort's estate, as was required by law. For this oversight, she was fined the exorbitant amount of £500 and given an extension of six months to carry out her obligation.[12]

Out of sight, out of mind, Sarah had happily settled into her new life with Kidd and the details of her past life with Oort were a distant memory. Kidd paid off all of John Oort's debts to eliminate Sarah's embarrassment, and he and James Emott, Kidd's lawyer and friend, successfully helped Sarah regain her inheritance from Cox. It may be that Sarah didn't think to inventory Oort's estate because Oort lived in *her* house among *her* things. Under the law, however, things that belonged to her were legally Oort's.[13] Eighteen months after Oort's death—the last possible date she could file without receiving another penalty—Sarah organized the exhibition of the inventory, and it was recorded on October 26, 1692.[14] With Kidd by her side, Sarah dipped her quill pen into a pot of black ink and signed the closing document of her brief marriage to John Oort with her mark, "SK," because she could not write her name. Then, she likely collected all the displayed items and put them back in her house where they belonged.

Around 1692, Sarah gave birth to a daughter, Elizabeth, and in 1694 she had another daughter, little Sarah.[15] During the colonial period, giving birth was a social and bonding event where women looked after one another. Sarah's babies would have been born at home in a separate area away from the main living quarters. Men were not involved in the birthing process, so Captain Kidd would have been busy elsewhere. It was the job of women—relatives, neighbors, friends, and elders in the colony—to act as midwives to assist in the delivery. Special birthing linens were prepared and laid out. Sarah would have used a birthing stool or perhaps a loved one held her upright and supported her as she progressed through labor. In the early stages, Sarah would have acted as the hostess of the festive occasion. It was an old English tradition for new mothers to serve "groaning cakes"[16]—a sweet nutritious baked good made of spices, molasses, rum, apples, and carrots—and "groaning beer." Sarah may have learned her recipe from her mother or from the women in the community who assisted her. As they waited for the blessed moment, the women would entertain themselves with gossip, jokes, and stories.

A practical how-to reference guide from 1675, *The Gentlewomans Companion or, A Guide to the Female Sex* suggests a homemade cordial of herbs, spices, and wine to facilitate the delivery. The book would have been familiar to English women in the colony. Its author, Hannah Wooley, was the first woman in England to earn her living by writing and her work was popular around the time Sarah was born in 1670. Sarah's mother may have received the recipe for "How to order a Woman with Child, before, in, and after her Delivery" when she gave birth to Sarah. And it's likely that Sarah's own midwife made a batch of this concoction to "give speedy ease" to her delivery. The recipe reads:

Take three or four drops of the distilled Oyl [oil] of Nutmegs in a spoonful of White-wine or take white Dictamn-root, stones of Dates, and Borax, of each two Scruples [a Scruple is a very small measure of weight of about 20 grains]; Cinamon, Cassia-Lignea, Amber, fine Pearl, of each one Scruple, Saffron half a Scruple, make a small powder of these, and divide them into two equal parts, and let her take the one part in a draught of Lilly-water, or Ale-posset made of Rhenish-wine. To the other part let her take in like manner six hours after it need require. If she be subject to swooning or fainting before or after labor give her a spoonful of this excellent Cordial.[17]

Sarah was very fortunate that she and her two daughters survived childbirth. The risks were very high for complications, and many women and children died during or after childbirth. With the joyous thought of new life there was always the imminent fear of death. Pious women turned to God for strength and prayed for a safe conclusion to their pregnancy. Some even wrote spiritual testaments.[18] Every pregnancy brought the same feelings and fears because there was such a lack of medical training for difficult deliveries and prenatal care.

There is no record of how Sarah felt about finally becoming a mother in her early twenties with her third husband, but it is very possible that she thought about her own mother during the process. It was an experience they both shared. Sarah may have been curious to know her mother's pregnancy history—did she lose a child? Were her pregnancies difficult? Did her own mother (Sarah's grandmother) help her during this important time?

A woman of Sarah's social standing enjoyed a "laying in" period of up to two weeks to recuperate from the birth and if she was interested and able, she nursed her babies for about a year. Sarah had Dorothy Lee and maybe Moll to help her look after the children, but she would have been the primary caregiver for her children's basic needs making sure they were fed, cared for if they were sick, and that their clothes were darned.[19] Sarah did not go back to work at the shop after Kidd helped her receive her inheritance from Cox. With Kidd away at sea, she was a full-time mother.

There were few schools in the American colonies and most children were taught to read or write at home. Reading and writing did not go hand in hand, they were separate skills. So, while a young girl may have been taught how to read, learning to write was reserved for the male members of the family and sons learned from their fathers.[20] Sarah knew how to read but she did not know how to write. It was not for lack of intellect on her part, but lack of access at a time when female literacy was not prioritized. Sarah taught her daughters by example how to manage a home and when they were old enough to understand, they would quickly learn that their mother was very astute and business savvy. This was no more evident than when Sarah and Kidd sold some of their properties—the Wall Street house (£130), the lot on King Street (£50), and the lot on Dock Street to Robert Livingston for £150 so he could build a new private dock.[21] It was clear that Sarah understood the nuances of land transactions. She was so confident, in fact, that she stood by Kidd's side at the municipal office and marked her initials, pledging that she signed the business transactions "freely and of her own accord without threats or compulsion of her husband."[22]

In the spring of 1692, the Irishman Colonel Benjamin Fletcher arrived as the new governor of New York to replace Henry Sloughter, who died suddenly after an extended bout of drinking. Sloughter had been in office only about a year, and that wasn't nearly enough time to quell the social divisions that developed during Leisler's Rebellion. Fletcher found New York even worse off than he'd anticipated. The economy was depressed and heavily in debt due to mismanagement and the extraordinary burdens of England's war with France.[23] Not only did the cost of the war severely impact the colony, the French had blocked the trade routes of the North Atlantic, leaving New York ships laid up and merchants struggling to engage in commerce. He reported that the people of New York were impoverished and in despair.[24]

The governor was ambitious and eager to make a name for himself by restoring New York's ailing economy. If he was successful, he thought, the Crown's coffers would be replenished and he might benefit financially as well. Knowing that thousands of pirates hoisted the black flag and prowled the seas attacking merchant vessels bound for the West Indies, West Africa, and North America Fletcher decided to use their illegal activity to his economic advantage. He would use their unlawful trade to help stimulate New York's economy. Fletcher's economic recovery plan entailed a simple change in attitude toward the pirates. Instead of fearing them, he would make New York City a safe place for pirates to visit and unload their stolen loot.

But who really were these men causing turmoil on the seas? And how did they shape New York's fate? Before we continue with Sarah's story, let's quickly delve into the lives of these notorious seafarers and the dramatic legacy they've left behind.

6

The Golden Age of Piracy

The British Crown had an empire to run, and they taxed the colonies to help them run it. They applied merchantilist doctrine to colonial trade by imposing Navigation Acts, which restricted what the colonies could manufacture, whose ships they could use, and with whom they could do business. As an incentive for American colonists to buy British goods, as opposed to French, Spanish, or Dutch products, the authorities passed these and other trade acts to require that all imported goods go by way of England.[1] These laws added enormously to the cost of imported goods, created a shortage in gold and silver coins, and depressed the market for North American goods abroad.

For colonial merchants, it was nearly impossible to survive economically under the rules established by the Crown. They took matters into their own hands by smuggling goods to Europe. To facilitate their illegal activity they built wharves and warehouses and commissioned the construction of boats (ketches, barques, and sloops) to sail to faraway ports.[2] To secure their fundamental interests, merchants took measures to maintain relationships with highly placed individuals in England, and they actively dominated the colonial councils.[3] But as the economy continued to flounder, colonists and merchants grew angry and desperate. The climate was ripe for piracy.

Known by many names—pirates, freebooters, sea rovers, Brethren of the Coast, or buccaneers—the men who turned pirate did not engage in maritime thievery just for the sport; there were reasons why they chose a dangerous but free life over one of stability and servitude. Many pirates were young unemployed deep-water sailors, others were fishermen or engaged in various trades on land, some were even soldiers in the militia. Most, but not all, were from the lowest rungs of society, poor and uneducated. The common assumption about pirates is that they were radically individualistic, scornful of the common ties that bind society together. In the words of the French historian Hubert Deschamps, pirates were:

> born of the sea and of a brutal dream, a free people, detached from other human societies and from the future, without children and without old people, without homes and without cemeteries, without hope but not without audacity, a people for whom atrocity was a career choice and death a certitude of the day after tomorrow.[4]

Why did these men turn pirate? Some did so out of revenge against merchant and naval ship captains who wielded a violent and arbitrary authority against them.[5] Pirates detested the strict social order meted out by the maritime martinets who made their lives so difficult. The naval and merchant captains were cruel and sadistic men who used brutal measures to enforce discipline on their crew.[6] Flogging with a cat-o'-nine-tails, sometimes six or seven hundred lashes, happened regularly. The sailor getting punished had to make the cat-o'-nine-tails himself by unwinding a rope into three strands, then further unwinding and knotting each strand. Fabric covered the top to make a long handle about a foot long giving the whipper a long range of motion. Each cat-o'-nine tails was used only once because its cords would get bloody and infect the wounds of the inflicted. Keelhauling, pulling seamen underneath the ship from one side to the other often resulting in their early death by drowning, was another common practice. Devastating diseases such as scurvy, dysentery, and syphilis were rampant on board merchant vessels, and these diseases spread quickly in the cramped quarters. Miserable food like hardtack biscuits infested with weevils, along with putrid water, and disabling accidents from shipboard mishaps or drunken brawls, were a way of life. And merchant sailors were given pittance for pay. Given the appalling conditions of merchant ships and few other options for unemployed mariners, piracy was an attractive alternative. By turning pirate these men could turn the tables: now *they* were the ones determining the fate of the captured merchant ship captain and his cargo, a decision based on the perceived character of the captain and the ship owner.[7] If the pirate captain believed the merchant captain had been decent to his crew, his life and his crew and cargo were spared. But if he had been cruel (the crew usually reported this to the pirates) he was punished as befitted his crimes. Pirates demanded fair and decent treatment of sailors because they had once been sailors themselves.

Turning pirate, for these men, was a distinct rejection of the life they once knew. It was an "alternative mode of life"[8] as one pirate described it. "Going on the account," a term that meant that payment was a share of the plunder rather than monthly wages,[9] attracted seafarers with the hope of making a fortune to support themselves or their families[10] or as a means of survival when trade opportunities declined.[11] One pirate said that he believed "most of the [pirate] Company came to get Money, but not to kill, except in Fight, and not in cold Blood."[12] Another pirate said he and the majority of his fellow pirates went rogue for "the love of drink and a lazy life" and these were "stronger motives than gold."[13] A victim of the pirates claimed that when he was captured, the men tried to entice him into the pirate life by promising him "If you will go with us on the Account, you shall have good Quarters and fare."[14]

Piracy also offered men an unheard-of level of freedom. Pirates were tolerant of differences in race, religion, and nationality and turning pirate was a chance for the oppressed of the late seventeenth century, Black or white, to live a better life.[15] As pirate captain Bartholomew Roberts said:

In an honest service: there is thin Commons, low Wages, and hard Labour: in this, Plenty and Satiety, Pleasure and Ease, Liberty and Power; and who would not balance Creditor on this Side, when all the Hazard that is run

for it, at worst, is only a sower Look or two at choak-
ing. No, *a merry Life and a short one*, shall be my Motto.[16]

Pirates contributed to the emerging economies of North
America by bringing in much-needed gold and silver coins
stolen from prizes. They also brought foodstuffs and luxury
items from faraway places that the colonists were eager to
purchase. Because the pirates had little overhead, they sold
their goods cheaply to the merchants, enabling them to turn
a nice profit. Pirates also purchased supplies and services from
the merchants, so the merchants made money from the pirates in this way, too.[17] Several colonies, particularly the Ba-
hama Islands, New York, Pennsylvania, Rhode Island, and
South Carolina, favored the pirates because their operations
gave lucrative employment to local mariners, shipbuilders,
craftsmen, and suppliers.[18]

The pirates were needed and appreciated so they were
not thought of as bandits or outlaws but as heroes. This cast
piracy in a different light—it was a solution to the trade
problem created by the British authorities and pirates were
providing services to the colonists. For men desperate for
work and on the fence about whether to turn pirate, this attitude toward piracy was a convincing tipping point.

Piracy is one of the most gendered forms of criminal activity and it attracted thousands of men and even some boys.[19] It
is estimated that about 25 to 30 percent of pirate crews were
Black and the majority of Black pirates were men who had
escaped slavery.[20] There were so many pirates active from
about 1650 to 1725 the period became known as the Golden

Age of Piracy. It is estimated that some 4,500 to 5,500 men went "on the account."[21]

One of the earliest glimpses into pirate life was written by the pirate surgeon John Exquemelin, also known as Alexander Oliver Exquemelin,[22] who presented in his book, *The Buccaneers of America*, a firsthand account of life among the pirates from the time he joined the buccaneers[23] in 1669 in Tortuga until 1674.[24] Written and published in Dutch in 1678 and later translated into English in 1684, Exquemelin's book was then, and still is, one of the most important source books on seventeenth-century pirates. Exquemelin described the pirates' highly organized democratic and civilized society on board ship and at the pirate islands of Tortuga and Hispaniola. The guarantees of civility and democracy were contained in the ship's articles that detailed all aspects of life on board the pirate ship. The ship's articles were a list of rules that spelled out the rights and obligations of crew members and were the foundation of the pirates' invented radical government.

Every man who joined the pirates was required to take an oath and commit to the articles by signing his name, or making his mark if he was illiterate, in the steward's book.[25] The ship's articles united men from many nations and who spoke many languages and made them a brotherhood that worked together for the good of the pirate society. The articles stated that members of the buccaneer commonwealth were expected to "be civil to one another, to aid their fellows in time of want, and to preserve the booty of dead pirates for their 'nearest relations' or their 'lawful heirs.'"[26] That last point—"to preserve the booty of dead pirates for their 'nearest relations' or their 'lawful heirs'"—is very important because although the pirates had their own commonwealths on the wooden decks of their ships and on land in their pirate colonies, the articles make it clear that their community extended beyond these boundaries, and that these ties were not only respected, but financially accounted for.

Exquemelin was the first source to mention the agreement between pirates to care for each other's relations in the event of their death. The agreement, called matelotage, is a partnership between two pirates[27] to pool all their possessions. "The pirates draw up a document, in some cases saying that the partner who lives longer shall have everything, in others, that the survivor is bound to give part to the dead man's friends or to his wife, if he was married."[28]

The pirates created a society for themselves that was a deliberate contradistinction of the life they knew on merchant and naval vessels. Their world was democratic. The pirate ship was a business and the crew members were co-owners.[29] A hierarchy with elected officers existed, but everyone was given a vote; this system provided order in the pirate community, not chaos as the authorities claimed. The articles outlined the responsibilities of the captain and the quartermaster, who were usually selected "over a bowl of punch."[30] The captain was chosen for his superior knowledge of navigation and seamanship, as well as his ability to lead his men in battle or against troublemakers. A typical captain was either an officer from a West Indian privateer or a mate or boatswain from a merchant ship which had mutinied or been captured by pirates.[31] His tenure depended on maintaining the respect and goodwill of his men. If he lost their confidence, he could be outvoted and dismissed from his position.

The quartermaster was an able-bodied individual responsible for the discipline on board. He had authority over the whole company, except when the pirate ship was called to action; then, the captain maintained total command of the vessel. The historian Marcus Rediker wrote that the quartermaster was "part mediator, part treasurer, and part keeper of the peace."[32] He was the captain's right-hand man and often became the captain of the vessel that was captured next. As the keeper of the booty, he was one of the most valuable members of the crew.

These sophisticated operations anticipated nearly every need of the pirate community. The ship's articles allocated some of the booty for "health care" for the men wounded in action, and the rest as compensation for the crew. The larger shares of the booty went to those most vital to the operation: Exquemelin names the captain, the hunter (employed to get the food supply of meat, usually pork and turtle, for the ship), the surgeon, and the carpenter, but these often changed from ship to ship. The captain, who was voted in and out of office by all the members of the crew,[33] received the most, "four of five of the men's portions";[34] the surgeon, "200-250 pieces of eight for his medical supplies, according to the size of the ship"; the hunter earned 200 pieces of eight; and the carpenter, 100-150 pieces of eight for his work in repairing and fitting out the ship.[35]

Pirates cared so deeply about the well-being of their members that they wanted to make sure they were fairly compensated for their pain and disability, including special health care allowances. They would be compensated with money or enslaved workers. The loss of a right arm was paid 600 pieces of eight or six workers; the left arm, 500 pieces of eight or five workers; the right leg, 500 pieces of eight or five workers; the left leg was 400 pieces of eight or four workers; an eye was compensated for with 100 pieces of eight or one worker; and a finger, the same as an eye, 100 pieces of eight or one worker.[36] If a pirate suffered a severe internal injury, he would be compensated with 500 pieces of eight or five workers.[37] After the salaries and the compensation for the wounded were paid out, the rest of the booty was divided by as many men as were on the ship. With the exception of those that received special portions of the booty—the captain, the quartermaster, the surgeon, the hunter, and the carpenter—the men received equal shares, and the boys received half of a man's share.[38]

Exquemelin described the values the pirates upheld. He said honesty and loyalty were so important to the sustainability of the buccaneer commonwealth that it was determined that "To prevent deceit, before the booty is distributed everyone has to swear an oath on the Bible that he has not kept for himself so much as the value of a sixpence, whether in silk, linen, wool, gold, silver, jewels, clothes, or shot from the capture. And should any man be found to have made a false oath, he would be banished from the rovers, and never more be allowed in their company."[39] The pirates had human values such as honesty and loyalty that organized their pirate community, and one pirate captain articulated this when he stressed to his men that breaking the articles would be "ill Precedent, and of bad Consequence. If we take the liberty of breaking our Articles and Oath, then there is none of us can be sure of anything… Do not let us break the Laws that we have made our selves, and sworn to."[40]

As we will see after Fletcher's term as governor, the authorities took swift and harsh legal action against the pirates and painted them as the worst kind of villain.[41] In piracy cases, the king was considered the victim and it was expected that the judge would do the Crown's bidding in the war against the pirates.[42] An accused pirate was subjected to a trial designed to give the advantage to the prosecutor. The burden of proof was on the defendant.[43] As one legal scholar, James F. Stephen, described it, "If any assumption was made in court about the prisoner, it was not that he was innocent until the case against him was proved beyond a reasonable doubt, but that if he *were* innocent he ought to be able to demonstrate it for the jury by the quality and character of his reply to the prosecutor's evidence."[44] The accused pirates had no legal representation and had to conduct their own defense. Since the majority of men on trial were seamen with little or no education, they were not equipped to make a good case for themselves,[45] and for many pirates the trial ended nearly as soon as it began. Sometimes as soon as the next day, court transcripts were peddled on the street to satisfy the interests of curious readers. It is these men who were Fletcher's welcome visitors.

7

Fletcher's Friends

The new governor was on extremely friendly terms with pirates, especially those who pillaged the East Indies and the Red Sea. Thomas Tew, one of the most notorious, was repeatedly invited to dine with Fletcher at the beautifully appointed governor's residence inside the fort. Tew's wife and children lived in New York, and when he was in port, Fletcher and Tew were seen in public walking around town together or riding in Fletcher's coach.[1] They even exchanged presents.[2] Fletcher explained his relationship with the pirate in a letter dated December 24, 1698, to the Council of Trade and Plantations.

> As to my intimacy with Tew, the truth and whole truth of that poor affair is this. This Tew appeared to me not only a man of courage and activity, but of the greatest sense and remembrance of what he had seen of any seaman that I ever met with. He was also what is called a very pleasant man, so that sometimes after the day's labour was done, it was divertisement as well as infor-

mation to me to hear him talk. I wished in my mind to make him a sober man, and in particular to cure him of a vile habit of swearing. I gave him a book for that purpose, and to gain the more upon him I gave him a gun of some value. In return he made me a present which was a curiosity, though in value not much, and this is the sum total of the kindness that I am charged with; for as to his coming to my table (which I think was such as became me and was hospitable to all), I hope that will not stick upon me if you enquire what others have done and still do in that kind.[3]

Fletcher readily issued privateering commissions that quickly eased into piracy. He allowed pirates to enter New York harbor, dispose of their stolen loot, and refit for their next voyage without fear of legal consequences.[4] For his "hospitality" he charged the pirates £100 each for a pass guaranteeing them protection—and he pocketed the protection money.[5] For every ship Fletcher let in, it was said there were nine pirate vessels waiting to unload in the harbor.[6] Pirates filled the purses of tavern keepers, prostitutes, and retailers with hard currency from around the world, especially "Araby" gold and Spanish doubloons.[7] They brought in exotic goods like silk carpets, muslins, ivory fans, looking glasses, and teakwood chairs, and with little overhead, they sold them to merchants at rock-bottom prices.[8] The merchants in turn marked up the goods and made soaring profits of up to 400 percent. With their new wealth they bought houses or started new businesses contributing to the local economy.

A handful of Fletcher's shrewd New York merchant friends

cashed in on the pirate free-for-all by investing heavily in the illegal trade between New York and Madagascar, an island larger than Great Britain that had become an important rendezvous point for pirates off the coast of East Africa. Pirates hid in their settlement there and ventured out to raid ships in and around the Indian Ocean. Frederick Philipse, lord of the ninety-two-thousand-acre Philipsburgh Manor in Westchester, New York, was New York's wealthiest merchant and ship owner.[9] A carpenter by trade, he married the rich widow, Margaret Hardenbroeck, and became her business partner in a vast international shipping business.[10] He avoided the Navigation Acts by sending ships halfway around the world four times a year from New York to Madagascar to exploit a lucrative multibusiness operation with the rich Madagascar pirates. Philipse filled their tankards with rum and Madeira wine, and sold them sought-after provisions like shoes, hats, tobacco paper, bread, sugar, and lime juice (to prevent scurvy) at astronomical prices. A cask of wine, for example, worth about £19 in New York, sold for £300 in Madagascar.[11] On the return trip, his ship captains brought back Malagasy people to sell in New York. The workers were acquired by trading munitions and pirate loot with local African kings.[12] Retiring pirates were also part of the business operation. Men who had had enough of the pirate life and wanted to return to society were ferried back to the colonies for 100 pieces of eight (they had to supply their own food and beverage).[13] Philipse's ships participated in the mariner's mail service, which allowed the pirates to stay in touch with their families and friends in New York. His captains stopped at Ascension Island, a remote outpost in the Atlantic, for fresh supplies of turtle meat and dropped off and collected the mail left under a rock with a hole in it near the harbor. Then on the return trip, they caught more turtles and picked up and dropped off the mail again. (Turtles were easy prey for mariners and they were plentiful. On ship, the cook kept turtles alive on their backs in the hold until it was time to cook them. Soft-shelled turtle eggs were also a popular delicacy.)

According to one report, Fletcher's economic program was worth about £100,000 a year to the city (and a tidy sum for him).[14] Sarah and Kidd knew Governor Fletcher. Kidd was a legitimate trader and his ship the *Antigua* went in and out of the harbor during his runs to the Caribbean. Sarah would have seen pirates strutting along the waterfront, their stolen knee-length velvet coats tied with silk waistbands. Their swords and daggers had hilts set with sparkling gems of green, white, and red, and their stocks of pistols glimmered with mother-of-pearl. Some had their ears pierced and dangled Venetian ducats or Arabian gold.[15] Sarah may have purchased some of the fine furnishings in her home from merchants peddling the Red Sea pirates' exotic goods.[16]

Fletcher's goal was to rebuild New York's economy (and his own), and however it happened under his auspicious program would be good for the Crown, he believed. The war with France had stretched the Crown's finances to the limit. If New York was prospering, then the authorities in London would be pleased with his managerial style. He was right—the king was too busy with European affairs to be concerned with the issues of the transatlantic colonies, and he counted on Fletcher to oversee the day-to-day operations in New York.

During Fletcher's tenure, his dubious conception of free trade brought real prosperity to Manhattan. Sarah saw the visible progress take shape all around her. More buildings were built. Newly opened markets, like the one under the trees by the Old Slip between Hanover Square and the East River, allowed Sarah to shop for fresh meat on Tuesdays, Wednesdays, and Saturdays.[17] She saw the new streets of Pine and Cedar laid out nearby, and others above Wall Street.[18] And the colony became enriched when Fletcher persuaded the Philadelphian, William Bradford, to move to New York to fill the position of royal printer, a position he held for the rest of his long life and in which he produced the first New York newspaper, the *New York Gazette*.[19]

All the buccaneers walking the streets of Fletcher's New York reminded Kidd of his exciting past as a privateer. He loved the challenge of putting his skills to good use for the benefit of his country in time of war. It satisfied the thrill he felt of leading a crew of men for a worthy cause. Sarah knew he was restless.

Kidd had been honing his skills for most of his life. Born January 22, 1654, in Dundee, Scotland, he was the son of a Presbyterian minister.[20] He went off to sea as a young man and eventually found his way to the Caribbean, where he drifted from port to port with other restless young seamen looking for work.[21] Little is known about his early years but he eventually worked his way up to be the captain of a ship.[22] In the seventeenth century, this was no mean feat because work and life on a king's ship in the British Navy or merchant ship was harsh. In order to have survived, Kidd had to be physically strong to handle the hard labor. By becoming captain, it meant he knew how to navigate a ship by latitude and longitude, maintain order among his crew, do the paperwork associated with voyages that required reading and writing skills, and make the decisions about the ship's destination.

Kidd had been working as a merchant captain for five years, in large part so that he would not be away from Sarah and the children for more than a few weeks at a time. But he was a man of the sea and he needed and wanted a new privateering assignment. He was hoping to land his dream job—an assignment sponsored by the monarch. Kidd told Sarah he would be gone only a few months. He would be back by Christmas for sure.

In late May 1695, forty-one-year-old Kidd and his sidekick, Sarah's twenty-one-year-old brother, Samuel Jr., prepared the *Antigua* for the two-month voyage across the Atlantic to London. Traveling across the ocean was risky and dangerous. Kidd would need to rely on a passing ship for help if anything went awry. As they sailed out of the harbor, Sarah and the girls could see the sails of the *Antigua* fill and flutter, the bowsprit pointed toward London's River Thames. Looking back to shore, Kidd could quickly locate their house by citing the tall house with scrolled dormers and fluted chimneys. The Kidds' distinguished home was often a landmark used by captains seeking a mooring in Manhattan's harbor.[23] Looking back for a last glimpse of his beloved, Kidd didn't need landmarks, he knew where his mooring was. It was with Sarah.

8

London

Word spread quickly of Kidd's departure. Like every mariner's wife, Sarah became the "head of household" and mistress of the realm until he returned. She made the financial decisions to keep the family on budget; tended the garden; nursed the sick making tonics with homegrown herbs to cure most ailments;[1] supervised the help; made sure the clothes were sewn, mended, and laundered in the creek near Maiden Lane (the northernmost completed east-west street of the time)[2] and kept pace with her daughters, three-year-old Elizabeth and one-year-old little Sarah.

Kidd and Samuel Jr. reached England and rented rooms from Mrs. Sarah Hawkins, a distant relative of Sarah's who lived in Wapping, a humble maritime community in a suburb of London.[3] Kidd knew that he'd left Sarah with a heavy load of responsibility while he followed a whim and a dream. Shortly after he arrived in London in July 1695, he set out to find a maid to bring back with him to New York to be an extra pair of hands for Sarah. It is not known if this was

Sarah's request, or if it was Kidd's gesture to appease his guilty conscience.

Kidd met Elizabeth Morris, a woman willing to engage as an indentured servant in exchange for passage out of England, her freedom at the end of four years, and a "double set of apparel." Kidd thought he was hiring someone to work alongside Dorothy Lee. Little did he know what an important role Elizabeth Morris would play in their lives. For now, however, with that task off his list, the biggest challenge he foresaw was how Sarah was going to differentiate between the two Elizabeths in the house—there was Elizabeth her toddler daughter, and Elizabeth the maidservant. Both might come at the sound of her voice.

While in London, Kidd met up with Colonel Robert Livingston, the Albany merchant who attended Leisler's hanging with Kidd. Livingston was in London on business to protect his interests in the East India Company—the British trading company made up of merchants who invested in trade in the East Indies. Kidd and Livingston's encounter thousands of miles away from New York was purely coincidental. Kidd told Livingston his reason for being in London. Livingston thought Lord Bellomont, soon to be the governor of New York, Massachusetts, and New Hampshire, might be able to help him find a privateering assignment. As a newly appointed colonial governor, Bellomont clearly had contacts in high places. Livingston arranged for the two to meet.

Kidd visited Bellomont three times at his house on Dover Street in London.[4] In a portrait of Bellomont from the era, he was a well-dressed, wigged gentleman with high-arched eyebrows, beady eyes, and a pointy chin. Compared to Kidd's muscular build, Bellomont was portly, with small, effeminate hands.[5] At each visit with Bellomont, Livingston accompanied Kidd and did all the negotiating. Bellomont later relayed Livingston's role to the secretary of state, James Vernon.

This detail proved important; Kidd was left out of the dealings; he was seen as the workhorse and they were the statesmen making the deal. The chain of authority was established early. Kidd learned that the sixty-two-year-old Lord Bellomont was a cash-strapped Irish peer. His wife, Countess Kate Bellomont, had extravagant spending habits and her gambling debts put great financial pressure on him.[6] Even though he had the fancy title of Captain General and Governor-in-Chief of His Majesty's Provinces of New York, Massachusetts, and New Hampshire, the job didn't pay much, at least not enough to support his wife and family in the colonies where things were more expensive, especially in New York.[7] Kidd's interest in obtaining a privateering commission and Bellomont's need for money intersected. Bellomont devised a plan.

Bellomont knew the king was keen to rid the seas of the pirates that were harassing the treasure-rich ships of the East India Company sailing in the Caribbean, Indian Ocean, and Red Sea. And he knew that England's war with France was straining their naval resources to the limit. A privateer could help with both problems. Bellomont's idea was a sort of get-rich-quick scheme that would please the king and make him rich.

Bellomont made all of the arrangements. Kidd was issued a privateering commission. As long as he stuck to French enemy ships, he was legal in the eyes of the law. But if he strayed toward other ships, he would be considered a pirate. Admiralty law required that if Kidd captured a French enemy ship, he had to verify the legality of it by obtaining from the ship's captain the vessel's registration called a French Pass. This proved to the authorities, and to Bellomont and his investors, that the ship was a lawful capture.

Kidd had years of experience as a privateer and his backers were confident he would make them rich. They were so sure of Kidd's ability that they gave him an additional assignment: pirate hunter. Since Governor Fletcher's courtship with the pirates to aid the New York economy, the government's policy toward pirates had changed. The colonial authorities wanted the lawlessness on the high seas stopped. They were fed up with the damage to commerce and the great loss of revenue to the Crown and merchants around the world. The colonial authorities hated them so much they branded them with an image that instilled fear and disgust calling them "worse than ravenous beasts."[8] Pirates were known as *hostes humani generis*, antisocial villains who were the "enemies of the human race."

Several pirates in the Red Sea were particularly troublesome to British trade. The most notorious were Thomas Tew—Governor Fletcher's frequent dinner guest—John Ireland, Thomas Wake, and William Maze.[9] They had joined forces in September 1695 with the pirate Captain Henry Avery of the *Fancy*. Avery was a distinguished-looking man. Tall, strongly built with a dark complexion and gray eyes, he wore a light-colored wig.[10] With Tew, Ireland, Wake, and Maze each sailing their own ship, they formed a small pirate squadron and attacked the Mocha fleet in the Red Sea.

The Mocha fleet was owned by the Grand Mugal Aurangzeb, emperor of the Muslim country of India and he was outraged when Avery and his pirates plundered the *Ganj-i-sawai* and the *Fath Mahmamadi*. The ships carried hundreds of pilgrims to Mecca and great amounts of gold and silver, elephant tusks, quicksilver, aloe, myrrh, frankincense, saffron, almonds, dates, and other fruit from trading with the Turks, Arabs, and Armenians.[11] Passengers were tortured, women raped, and the stolen treasure of about £200,000 amounted to nearly twenty million pounds in today's dollars.[12] The Grand Mugal held the East India Company liable for Avery's atrocities; he was outraged that their heavily armed ships patrolling in the Indian Ocean did not protect the Mocha fleet. This caused considerable damage to England's relations with the Grand Mugal and efforts were made to capture Avery but he escaped never to be seen again. Tew, Ireland, Wake, and Maze were still at large, however, and this is where Kidd was especially well qualified for this assignment. As a master mariner, he knew the pirates and where they rendezvoused.

Kidd's two privateering commissions were not the typical letters of marque. Imagining the potential for great profits if Kidd succeeded at his missions, some of the most powerful men in England formed a syndicate to sponsor Kidd's voyage.[13] His backers included four prominent members of the Junto (as the Whig ministry was called)—Lord John Somers, Keeper of the Great Seal of England; the Earl of Romney, lord lieutenant of Ireland; the Earl of Shrewsbury, secretary of state; and the Earl of Orford, first lord of the Admiralty. Also two wealthy merchants, the director of the East India Company, Edward Harrison, and Sir Richard Blackham.

Kidd, Lord Bellomont, Livingston and the king were in on the deal.[14] The total investment was about £50,000.[15]

What made this arrangement unusual was not only the high-profile members who invested, but the special dispensation they gave themselves from the normal privateering terms. The syndicate would have exclusive ownership of all the goods Kidd might seize[16] and waived the requirement that all prizes be declared at the British Admiralty Court. The Admiralty normally took 15 percent of the prize money. In bypassing the Admiralty Court, they planned to keep all the profits for themselves. It was agreed that the profits would be distributed as follows: Kidd and his men would take not more than 25 percent; the king received 10 percent and the nine partners would share 65 percent.[17] Kidd was offered a lucrative incentive by receiving the ship outright if the profits exceeded £100,000 and a return on his investment of 10 percent.[18]

Bellomont wrote the sailing orders instructing Kidd to "serve God in the best Manner you can" and to "sail directly to Boston to deliver unto me the Whole of what Prizes, Treasure, Merchandizes, and other Things, you shall have taken by virtue of the Power and Authorities granted you."[19] He also arranged a financial agreement with Captain Kidd and Robert Livingston whereby Lord Bellomont was the primary investor in one share of the privateering expedition owning four-fifths of the share, and Captain Kidd and Robert Livingston each owned one half of the fifth part.[20] Bellomont was not only Kidd's employer, he was his business partner.

Kidd was reluctant to take the job, probably because of the harm it would do to several New York acquaintances who supplied goods to the Madagascar pirates, but Livingston and Lord Bellomont talked him into it by playing to his vanity. They told him he was the only man who could accomplish the mission and that his stellar reputation and skills could not be replicated. When he hesitated, Bellomont threatened him saying that if he did not go on the voyage, he would stop the *Antigua* in the River Thames and make it impossible for her to clear for America.[21] This would mean his return to Sarah would be delayed indefinitely. Kidd described Bellomont's hard sell at his house on Dover Street:

> The Lord Bellomont told me he was to be Governor of New York, as well as of New England, and would protect me from any charge or accusation to be brought against me; and that he had powerful friends in the Government, who would not let me suffer any damage or prejudice either in England, or elsewhere. I, not withstanding, pressed to be excused, and to pursue my voyage to New York; whereupon the Lord Bellomont added threats to his wheedles, and told me I should not carry my own ship out of the river of Thames, unless I would accept the command of the ship to be fitted out.[22]

Kidd was under pressure to give them an answer. There was no way he could communicate with Sarah in a timely fashion to get her opinion and approval. He knew she trusted him to make the right decision. Kidd accepted the privateering job, but sensing his reluctance, Livingston took him on a tour of the great houses belonging to his investors, the Lords Somers, Romney, Russell, and the Duke of Shrewsbury "for my satisfaction that those great men were concerned in the expedition…but would not suffer me to see or speak with any of them," Kidd said.[23]

Kidd was reassured of their support and Bellomont confirmed he would be free of criminal prosecution telling Kidd that:

> the noble lords…should stifle all complaints that should be made in England, and he himself would prevent all clamours in those parts where he was Governor but condemning all the goods and treasure I should bring in, and disposing of them privately, and satisfying the owners for such part as should be due to them.[24]

Kidd signed the agreement on October 10, 1695.[25] His dream had come true, he'd received the monarch-sponsored assignment he'd been hoping for. The letters of marque were imprinted with the royal seal of the king of England. Once committed, Kidd had to come up with his share of the investment. He sold the *Antigua*—the ship he sailed for six years—to raise cash. The *Antigua* was his one connection to home and Sarah. He'd been sailing it when he and Sarah reconnected, and it was his livelihood during their first five years of marriage. Kidd still needed more money. His bond was set at £20,000 and Livingston had to back this up with a bond for £10,000.[26] To secure the bond with Livingston, he needed to put as collateral the property he owned before marrying Sarah, 86-90 Pearl Street, should he not fulfill his assignment.[27] Kidd felt certain that would never happen.

9

Provisioning in New York

In July 1696 Kidd returned to New York. Sarah was expecting Kidd to sail into New York harbor in the *Antigua* but instead he commanded a 287-ton newly built warship with three tall masts, square-rigged sails, and thirty-four big guns. It was a hybrid ship called a galley meaning that it could be rowed as well as sailed. Forty-six sweeps, or oars, on the lower deck propelled the vessel when the wind was too strong or it was too calm to sail.[1] A similar galley from the period, the *Charles*, could do three miles an hour with three men on each oar.[2] Launched at Castle Yard, Deptford, England, it was registered under the name the *Adventure Galley*.[3] On board was Elizabeth Morris and Samuel Jr., now a year older and a sunburned, seasoned sailor.

Sarah had never seen some of the men who disembarked from the *Adventure Galley*. Kidd explained that they were acquired involuntarily as he was leaving the River Thames. His ship was stopped and the king's officers impressed some of Kidd's best crew to serve in the British Navy to fight the French. Kidd, with letters of marque in hand, contacted his important investors and the situation was resolved. Some of his men were returned to him, but not all. A few new sailors were added to Kidd's roster but with only seventy men, he was still short a good number to successfully man the 124-foot ship.

Kidd had so much to tell Sarah about his acquisition of the *Adventure Galley* and his new position as a privateer. He explained that Lord Bellomont had wanted him to go straight to Madagascar from London to hunt pirates at Saint Marie, an island off Madagascar's east coast and the primary hangout for around fifteen hundred Red Sea pirates, but Kidd wanted to detour home to New York to see Sarah and the children. And while he was there, he could attend to important business—he needed to recruit more crew for his voyage.

Kidd showed Sarah his two commissions, the letters of marque, one signed by the king himself, William III. She'd easily recognize her king in the etching in the left top corner of the scrolled parchment.[4] Kidd explained that he had been given the extra assignment of pirate hunter because, as an experienced privateer, he knew the pirates' haunts and had a thorough knowledge of them.[5] He would be at war against the pirates. He may have also shared the fact that the king particularly liked that he was a family man with a wife and children.

As Sarah listened, she silently transitioned out of her dual role of master of the house and mistress of the realm to just mistress of the realm. And no doubt it took some readjusting. Not only would she have to make emotional (and physical) room for him again, but she'd also relinquish his position back to him as the head of the family. Sarah also had to adapt to his timeline. She thought he was going to be home by Christmas at the latest. He was six months late. She had spent Christmas and the girls' birthdays without him. Elizabeth was now four and little Sarah was two years old. Sarah herself had had a birthday too, of course, and she was now twenty-six years old. Kidd was forty-two.

Kidd explained that finding a privateering job and setting up his business arrangement was complicated. It had taken longer than he expected. Perhaps, in that moment, Sarah suddenly felt a deep connection with her mother, who had also faced days and nights alone while her seafaring husband was gone.

While Kidd was in London, a life-changing event for Sarah began to take shape. Plans were underway for the construction of the city's first English house of worship, Trinity Church, on the corner of Broadway and Wall Street. Sarah had been attending services in the chapel erected in the fort near the Battery for many years but with the support of Governor Fletcher, a staunch Anglican, the English community would finally have their own house of worship. In a letter to the archbishop of Canterbury, the vestry described the site as situated "very pleasantly upon the banks of Hudson's river," with "a large cemetery on each side, enclosed on the front by a painted paled fence."[6]

Twelve men, the "apostolic band," organized the effort and one of them was Sarah and Kidd's attorney and friend, James Emott. Each founder was responsible for contributing money and for locating materials and labor. As many as 20 percent of New Yorkers in the colonial period were enslaved

Africans.[7] Some of the founders "volunteered" their enslaved workers to labor in the construction of Trinity Church, the newest site for religious expression. In the blistering hot sun, these men toiled to build the rectangular stone structure with a high mansard roof and a small entrance porch.[8] The only place for them to escape the sweltering heat was shade from the newly planted lime trees that lined the fence.[9]

On July 19, 1696, just days after Kidd returned to New York, he walked with James Emott to see the construction site of Trinity Church. Knowing of Sarah's deep faith,[10] and her commitment to regular religious ritual, Kidd wanted to help provide a spiritual home for Sarah and the girls. The notes from the first recorded meeting regarding the building of Trinity Church taken in 1696 state that Kidd "lent a Runner & Tackle for the hoisting up Stones as long as he stays here."[11] Kidd knew that his contribution, while not insignificant, would be short-lived because he was quickly acquiring the necessary crew for his voyage. In a matter of weeks he would be using the runner and tackle to sail the *Adventure Galley* on his privateering voyage. Still, every little bit helped, and he mined all available resources, even selling oil from the whales that washed up on the colony's shores. (Whale stranding occurred so frequently in New York City that a procedure was established for disposing of the whales and marketing the valuable "oyle.")[12]

As was the custom of the day, members of the congregation rented pews. Sarah and Kidd were one of the initial pewholders and were assigned to pew number four. The pew was an open rectangular box with a small latched door that opened from the center aisle. They owned half of the pew and sat on bench seats or chairs. The church was not heated and ladies were encouraged to bring a foot stove, typically made of perforated metal or wood and filled with a box of hot coals, to warm themselves.[13] The Kidd pew was in a prominent location at the front of the church, where Sarah and her girls could see and hear the clergy and experience the teachings from the Book of Common Prayer. Those around her were some of the most respected members of the community.

Kidd and Sarah spent the rest of the summer together. They may have had dinner at a tavern on the East River where twice a week there was a turtle feast. Or, they may have played outside with their daughters, bowling on the grass near the street named for it, Bowling Green.[14] They likely entertained at home using their substantial quantity of dinnerware to entertain groups as large as a dozen. Details of Kidd's voyage would have distracted him from totally relaxing and Kidd likely gathered his officers and some of his crew in his home in preparation for the voyage. There was plenty of room for them to sit on the Kidds' four dozen chairs.

During August 1696 the hold of the *Adventure Galley* was loaded with cargo needed for the long voyage to the Indian Ocean. Each box, barrel, trunk, and sack had to be carefully placed for access and weight taking care not to put too many heavy things in the stern or the bow would ride high. Calculations were made to ensure there was enough food and water for each man. If the trip was delayed for any unforeseen reason, including threatening and debilitating weather, the men might run out of provisions and the voyage could be ruined if they were not able to make land and reprovision. The goal was to arrive in the Indian Ocean with a full crew, a heavy ask in seventeenth-century maritime life.

Kidd and Sarah were aware of how little time they had together. The tick of the clock in their home was a constant reminder. Still, Kidd had returned to Manhattan to see Sarah and he so enjoyed the luxurious comforts of his home. Sarah made sure the private living quarters were especially welcoming. She put quilts on the three beds—quilts that she likely stitched herself—and goose down pillows and bolsters.

By late August, the pace quickened because Kidd needed to depart on September 6 if he was to avoid bad weather and reach the Red Sea safely. Kidd took on an especially large crew to man the ship (he needed at least 100 men to work the cannon) and to sail any captured ships. He organized the 154 men along the lines of a navy ship with two watches: the larboard watch or "port" side (the left-hand side of the ship), and the starboard watch (right-hand side). The larboard watch was headed by Henry Mead who brought with him his fine beige waistcoat and twenty books to read. The starboard watch was led by twenty-six-year-old Dr. Robert Bradinham who doubled as the ship's surgeon.[15] John Walker had the most important assignment of quartermaster serving as Kidd's right-hand man in charge of the crew. William Moore was the gunner in charge of teaching the crew how to use the thirty-four big guns and Richard Barleycorn was Kidd's fourteen-year-old cabin boy apprenticed for six years. Samuel Jr. was assigned to the starboard watch. There were two father-son combinations. The majority of the men were young—poor restless spirits eager to take on a risky adventure. They chose dangerous work at sea over their previous land jobs as soldiers, farmers, cordwainers, gunsmiths, bakers, carpenters, and laborers because they believed the work held a potential for great riches. One servant, Saunders Douglas, was put on board by his master, New York City vintner Michael Hawden, so he could collect half of Douglas's share.[16] A few were experienced mariners, but not many. Two out of three were English and one out of six were Dutch.[17] There was a Jewish jeweler named Benjamin Franks from Jamaica who was using the *Adventure Galley* as his ride to get to India where there was the largest supply of precious stones.

Twelve of Kidd's crew members prepared for the voyage by obtaining from the merchant Joseph Blydenburgh their basic necessities: waistcoats, breeches, shirts, shoes, stockings, handkerchiefs, combs, thread, buttons, knives, spoons, rum, sugar, spices, tobacco, paper, and cash.[18] They borrowed up to £1500 on the promise that when they returned they would give Blydenburgh one third of their share of any "money, plate bullion, Negroes, gold, jewels, and silks" they obtained from the voyage.[19] This financial arrangement was common among privateers who could not collect their wages before the voyage. The bond was an upfront payment that provided for the immediate needs of the crew member and those of his family.

Kidd made clear to his men the terms of the contract for the voyage.[20] They agreed to work under the "no prey—no pay" agreement, sometimes called "no purchase—no pay." This meant that it was only *when* a prize was captured that a crewman "earned" his pay and that pay would be given at the end of the voyage. If they did not make any ship captures they went home empty-handed. The proportion that Kidd and the crew would share would not exceed one fourth of the entire take.[21] Once the total value of the captured booty was calculated and the costs of the voyage deducted, the participants were given their share. Kidd was allocated thirty-five shares, experienced mariners (this included Kidd's officers) received a full share and landsmen and boys received less than a full share, but not less than half a share. No one was allowed to keep plunder for themselves; all must be turned over and accounted for. If someone stole booty he lost his share. The heirs of any crew member who died received £20 even if there was no prey from the voyage. The man who spied the first sail of an enemy ship was rewarded 100 pieces of eight and if it was proved that a man was drunk or a coward during the line of duty he lost his compensation.[22]

Governor Fletcher had a low opinion of Kidd's crew. He thought it was a ragtag group and he didn't believe Kidd could keep them under control with the financial terms he offered them in the agreement. Two months before Kidd departed, in July 1696, Fletcher communicated to the Board of Trade in London his concern:

One Captain Kidd lately arrived here, and produced a commission under the Great Seal of England, for suppressing of piracy. When he was here many flocked to him from all parts, men of desperate fortunes and necessitous, in expectation of getting vast treasure... It is generally believed here they [the men] will have money "par fas et nefas" [one way or the other] if he miss of the design intended for which he has commission twill not be in Kidd's power to govern such a load of men under no pay.[23]

★ ★ ★

As Kidd made the final preparations for the voyage, Sarah made arrangements to move on board ship with him. They wanted to spend every last minute together. For a few days, she made Kidd's cabin in the stern of the ship *their* home. Sarah's interest in living on board ship shows her ease with that wooden world. She had crossed the Atlantic to get to the New World and it is very likely that as a mariner's daughter she had spent time at sea with her father, or at least knew her way around his ships. It is not known what part of England she hailed from, but in all likelihood it was a port city where her father conducted his business.

Kidd's crew gave them their privacy. Kidd's bunk was nothing compared to the four-poster canopy bed they shared on Pearl Street, but they didn't care. Sarah may have brought some things from home to make it more cozy. While he fitted out the ship, she organized his cabin, tending to the small details to make it like home. Sarah helped Kidd pack his sea trunk with his personal belongings. She folded his dressy waistcoat, and carefully stored away a tankard, plate, candlesticks, and quill pen and ink. Kidd stored the ship's papers in another trunk to make sure they stayed safe and dry. He kept a list of his crew members and the ship's articles, a document that detailed the rules of the ship signed by each man, usually with his mark—"X," and his two privateering commissions. Kidd's letters of marque, his journal to record the details of the voyage, and, if he obtained any, the French Passes, were the most important documents among his belongings.[24] Without these documents to support his activities, he could be accused of going rogue. It is very likely he also packed something personal from Sarah to keep her near while he was away. She probably gave him something special she loved like a linen handkerchief that smelled like her and had her initials cross-stitched with a number in the corner.

On September 6, 1696, the *Adventure Galley* was ready to sail. Kidd was in his element back at sea. He had a powerful warship at his command. He and his crew of more than 150 men were on a mission sponsored and financed by some of the most powerful men in England. The one-time merchant sea captain had reason to feel proud. He had bragging rights, although some in the city and on the docks complained about his arrogance and boisterousness as he flitted the facts of his monarch-sponsored privateer commissions in their faces. Sarah and the girls said their goodbyes to Kidd, who assured them he would be back in a year. They watched the *Adventure Galley* pull away from the dock and move into the great harbor. As a privateer, Kidd was permitted to fly the British Union Jack (called the king's jack) and naval pendant flags.[25] As Kidd's ship passed the fort, Sarah saw the flags fluttering in the wind and she heard salutes fired.[26] Kidd had his men trim the sails and pointed the bow toward Staten Island before heading to Sandy Hook and then the great wide expanse of the Atlantic Ocean. Kidd's departure had to have triggered a flood of emotions in Sarah: the love of her life, the father of her children, and her dear brother Samuel Jr. were on board that ship, sending their last signal to her. A nautical goodbye wave. Kidd may have shared with Sarah the route he was taking to the Indian Ocean. The quickest and safest way would be to head to the Madeira Islands off the west coast of Africa, then go south and sail around the Cape of Good Hope to Madagascar. Kidd was as fine a navigator as there was. He understood the trade winds, the monsoon season; he charted his course by the stars and the moon; he understood the tides. For all of his adult life he fearlessly sailed from one end of the globe to another. Sarah was confident he would find his way back to her. He promised her he would. His privateering contract was for one year and his deadline to return was Wednesday, March 25, 1697.

10

Waiting

After Kidd left in the fall of 1696, the Common Council agreed to make several key improvements to New York City.[1] An ordinance read that due to "the great inconveniency that attends this city, being a trading place, for want of having lights in the dark time of the moon in the winter season, it is therefore ordered that all and every of the housekeepers with this city shall put out lights in the windows fronting the respective streets of the city, between November and March 25 in the following manner: Every seventh house, in all the streets, shall, in the dark time of the moon, cause a lantern and candle to be hung out on a pole—the charge to be defrayed equally by the inhabitants of the seven houses."[2] A night watch was also established in which "four good and honest inhabitants of the city" would walk the streets from nine in the evening till break of day. These watchmen were to go around the city every hour with a bell and proclaim "the season of the weather and the hour of the night."[3] It would be easy for Sarah to remember the last day of the street lighting and the night watch programs because March 25, 1697, was the last day of her husband's privateering contract. Kidd would be home.

Yet on that day there was no sign of Kidd. He'd run into serious problems and was delayed. Many of his men had died from disease and he himself had contracted scurvy from lack of fresh food. In the year that he'd been gone, he had not seen a single pirate ship. By the end of that March, Kidd was nowhere near the North American coast, he was still in the Indian Ocean in the Comoros Islands northwest of Madagascar. What Sarah knew about Kidd's whereabouts is unclear, but she did know that per Kidd's contract, Lord Bellomont was expecting him in Boston. With so much uncertainty, Sarah may have heard her mother's voice echoing in the words of Ede Wilday, wife of Richard Wilday, a crewman on the *Adventure Galley*, who said one "must wait in patience for shipps to return."[4]

That winter in 1698 was one of the coldest on record in the Northeast. Sarah and the girls had the help of Elizabeth Morris and Dorothy Lee to stoke the fireplaces and warm the blankets. Despite the cold snap, things in the colony were changing: Fletcher was recalled from his post as governor of New York because the colony was not producing enough revenue. Bookkeepers in London overseeing the colony's cash flow realized that a large amount of money was going straight into Fletcher's pocket. His time governing the newly counted population of nearly five thousand, the majority of them white and seven hundred of them Black, was over.[5]

That March, in the dawn of spring, Trinity Church finally opened. To the devout Sarah this was the kind of exciting news she would have shared with Kidd. Through James Emott, a vestryman and a generous supporter of Trinity, Sarah would have swapped Kidd updates.[6] But another year passed, and on March 25, 1698, there was still no sign of Kidd.

Lord Bellomont arrived in New York April 2, 1698, to great fanfare as the new governor. A zealous member of the Whig party in the House of Commons, he was rewarded for his loyalty to the king with this appointment. Intent on being a new and different administrator from his predecessor, Benjamin Fletcher, he immediately declared that New York was going to become morally upright and that cursing, drinking, lewd conduct, and Sabbath breaking would not be tolerated. His stand as a law and order governor intent on suppressing piracy won favor with King William but raised eyebrows among the merchants used to Fletcher's loose (or nonexistent) regulations and easy payoffs.[7] His posture that piracy was an "abomination" and that it was "not only injurious to the Honour of his Majesty, and the English Nation, but also highly prejudicial to the Trade of England, and particularly to the East India Company"[8] ruffled the feathers of merchants in the community who benefitted from the cheap and exotic goods the pirates supplied. Sarah may have heard the gossip in the shops from tradespeople used to the old ways.

Sarah knew Kidd's agreement with Bellomont was to return directly to Boston. She turned to her trusted friend and Kidd's lawyer, James Emott, for assistance. He had helped her gain her inheritance from Cox and now she wanted him to represent her to Lord Bellomont and ask him if he would

grant Kidd permission to return to port in New York instead
of Boston to reunite with his family sooner.[9]

Sarah's request shows her bold confidence and resourceful-
ness. She knew who to turn to and what she wanted Emott
to do for her. Every day she looked for Kidd's ship in the
harbor and she may have imagined their reunion after so
much time apart. Warm memories of their last summer together as a family and their private moments on board ship
before the voyage. The inefficient use of time, energy, and
resources to go to Boston first just would not do for the lo-
gistically organized Sarah Kidd. Sarah knew her husband
would want this arrangement too. Traveling to Boston to
meet with Bellomont could add weeks to their separation.
Her request reveals how savvy she was as head of household
and mistress of the realm; she was always thinking how best
to keep her family together and her marriage alive.

Bellomont agreed.[10] His voyage from England to New
York to take up his post as governor had been fraught with
mishaps causing his ship to sidetrack to Barbados for repairs.
After a long and arduous journey, Bellomont was amenable
to staying put in New York until Kidd's return.

By June, those aboard returning ships from Madagascar
were spreading rumors and gossip about Kidd and his crew
on the *Adventure Galley*. Wives of Kidd's crew wrote letters
to their husbands aboard the *Adventure Galley* through the
mariner's mail service. The regularity of trading ships carrying mail between New York and Madagascar made it possible for men to stay in touch with their families while they
were at sea. A letter from Sarah Horne of Flushing, New
York, to her husband, Jacob Horne, was found in the mail-

bag of a captured merchant ship seized by a British privateer for trading with pirates. The undelivered letter from Captain Samuel Burgess's ship, the *Margaret*, is preserved in the Admiralty Papers in The National Archives in London. It confirms that she and Jacob had exchanged letters. She informed him that she'd heard distressing rumors about Kidd's voyage: "I have heard an abundance of flying news concerning you,"[11] she wrote. Sarah's letters to Kidd have not survived, but it is very possible that Sarah warned Kidd about the gossip in Manhattan. Trouble was brewing.

11

Emott's Secret

To Sarah's surprise, James Emott was at her door. He had rushed over from his house nearby, on the east side of Broadway just above Wall Street.[1] A messenger had just delivered a letter to him, unusual for a Saturday. The letter was urgent.[2] Her husband was back in home waters.

It had been three long years since Captain Kidd left on what was supposed to be a one-year voyage. From her parlor window, Sarah could scan the horizon for the distinctive features of her husband's missing ship. She knew the vessel like she knew her Pearl Street mansion. Now she saw hundreds of ships in the harbor with crewmen climbing the tall wooden masts, hoisting canvas sails and scrubbing the planked decks, but not one of them was the *Adventure Galley*.

Emott told Sarah that he had a secret to tell her and no one, *no one*, could know. Outside Sarah's three-story mansion on the corner of Pearl and Hanover Street a wide dirt road ran parallel to the harbor and city wall. It was a busy thoroughfare and anyone on foot or horseback could peer into the Kidds' large street-level windows. They could see who was inside and perhaps even catch snippets of conversation. Emott was a recognizable figure in the city, not only as an attorney, but for his leadership in the Trinity Church community. Manhattan was a gossip-ridden town. Anyone who might see Emott in Sarah's home could start a rumor that he was visiting the wife of the privateer who was several years past his return date. Some might speculate that the visit had to do with Captain Kidd, but others could promote a mischievous notion that there was something untoward between Emott and Sarah.

Emott needed a place to talk that was as safe as a vault. Up two flights of stairs there was an attic that doubled as a secure warehouse for the cargo Captain Kidd acquired when he worked as a merchant sea captain trading in the West Indies. Using a rooftop crane he hoisted wooden crates into the area the length and width of the house—thirty-eight feet across by forty-eight feet deep. The gabled roof formed a peak that was high enough to stand under, and the space was adequately lit by three dormered windows. Sarah would've used the attic to conduct clandestine conversations, away from public scrutiny. It's there where Emott likely told Sarah why her husband's ship was not in the harbor.

Kidd's letter came from Oyster Bay, New York, a small port named for its oyster-rich waters twenty-five miles from Manhattan on Long Island. Kidd chose to anchor there because he knew Justice White and Dr. Cooper, two of the town's prominent citizens, would help him send his letter and keep quiet about his whereabouts.[3] Kidd asked Emott to come immediately. His privateering voyage had gone terribly wrong: his men had mutinied, he was accused of mur-

dering a mutineer, ninety-seven of his men deserted him in
Madagascar, and the renegades spread rumors in every port
that Captain Kidd was a dangerous pirate.[4] Word had already
reached the authorities in London. With strong encourage-
ment from the East India Company—an English trading
company that produced Indian silks, calicoes, and muslins
in factories in the East Indies and whose ships were frequent
catnip for pirates—Britain's lords justices sent instructions to
all the colonial governors and sheriffs on the North American eastern seaboard to capture Captain Kidd whenever he
should appear.[5] Kidd needed Emott to help him prepare his
defense and act as an intermediary between him and Lord
Bellomont to secure a pardon.

It's clear that Emott believed Kidd's letter was genuine. It
was signed *"Wm. Kidd,"* the distinctive way Captain Kidd
signed his name. The paper was folded in thirds, sealed with
wax, and imprinted with Kidd's personal seal ring.[6] Sarah
could run her index finger over the wax impression to de-
termine if it really was from her husband.

Sarah understood why Captain Kidd contacted Emott instead of her. Their home on Pearl Street would be the first
place the authorities would look for him. Emott told Sarah
that until Captain Kidd's name was cleared and he was assured of a pardon from Lord Bellomont, she could be in
grave danger as an accessory to an accused pirate. In one
split second, Sarah's conventional marriage to Kidd turned
dangerous. At her husband's insistence, she and the children were to leave Manhattan immediately. Kidd had arranged for Sarah and the children to stay on Block Island, a
famous outlaw destination nine miles south of the mainland

of Rhode Island. She would be safe there with their good friends, Edward and Mary Sands, until he could rendezvous with her. She should pack as if going on a long trip. There was no telling when she would be able to return if Kidd didn't receive his pardon.

Sarah knew a great deal about Lord Bellomont, the man who now held her husband's fate in his hands. Bellomont's principle assignment as governor was to rid the colonies of pirates. New York, in particular, had been an accepting place for "free traders"—men who thought that others' trade goods were free for the taking. Dismantling the lucrative and deeply embedded pirate operations that had become a part of the New York culture would have been a tall order for any royally appointed governor, but for Bellomont, it was an especially complicated one.

Back when Kidd and Bellomont signed their financial agreement and secured the necessary letters of marque, it wasn't obvious that Bellomont's two roles as governor and investor would ever be in direct conflict with each other. Bellomont, as governor, was the Crown's man to stamp out piracy. As investor, he fully expected to secure his financial future. Bellomont did not anticipate that anything could go awry. Kidd trusted Bellomont and believed the confidence was mutual. But for Sarah, the strong directive to leave home immediately must have been deeply unsettling. Kidd's posture had changed from one of absolute trust in Lord Bellomont to one of caution.

Sarah's belief in her husband's judgment didn't seem to waver; she embraced the situation as a dutiful wife loyal to her husband and followed Emott's instructions to the letter. She gathered the children, seven-year-old Elizabeth and five-year-old little Sarah. She collected the valuables from around the house including extra money Emott said Kidd would need. She packed a tankard, a silver mug, silver porringers, spoons, forks, plates, clothes for herself and the children, at least 100 pieces of eight for Kidd and 260 pieces of eight from her own savings.[7] She stored them in a wooden trunk for easy transport. It was all she had, and with her future so uncertain, she would need every single piece of eight.

Sarah wanted company and an extra pair of hands to help with the luggage and the children. She asked her maid, Elizabeth Morris, to accompany her. Morris quickly packed a few things for herself, including her life savings of twenty-five English crowns, and put them in Sarah's traveling trunk.[8] Dorothy Lee would mind the Pearl Street residence while Sarah was away.

Sarah's secret departure to go meet Kidd on Block Island was not without its risks; her husband's life was in danger and so might be hers. She could only hope that she and her husband would return home soon and that they could go back to simpler times when hoisting crates of cargo onto the rough-hewn attic floor was the biggest event of the day.

Following Kidd's plan, Emott contacted Thomas Clark, a merchant friend of Kidd's and the former New York coroner, who had access to a boat and a secret warehouse in Stamford, Connecticut.[9] Clark was to ready the boat and transport Sarah to the safe location in Block Island Sound. She sent the trunk aboard, gathered her children, and departed in the waiting sloop.

Packing her silver and sending the trunk aboard Clark's

waiting vessel may have reminded her of her departure from England to the New World fifteen years ago. She learned then, at the age of fourteen, how to be brave when leaving the past behind. In addition to her silver collection were her most prized possessions, her young daughters. Sarah may have felt anxious about the gravity of the situation, but she would have been stoic and strong for the sake of her children whose fear no doubt showed through the tears in their innocent eyes.

12

Taking Precautions

Emott left Manhattan immediately. He traveled with the messenger by foot, ferry, and horseback to Oyster Bay, arriving one day after he received Captain Kidd's letter. He was rowed out to Kidd's sloop, the *Saint Antonio*, a small, swift, and heavily armed vessel loaded with treasure. Kidd purchased the *Saint Antonio* in Hispaniola to replace the *Adventure Prize*—once the *Quedah Merchant*—that was in disrepair. Emott reported that Sarah and the children were safe and had fled Manhattan on Thomas Clark's boat, just as Kidd had instructed in his letter. The two strategized how Kidd could clear his name and secure a pardon. They would need to find the closest and safest point near Boston, where Lord Bellomont was now residing.

While the shipmaster, John Ware, sailed the *Saint Antonio* for the one-hundred-mile trip down Long Island Sound to Boston, Kidd and Emott drafted a letter of defense that Emott could hand deliver to Boston's governor. Captain Kidd dropped Emott at Stonington, Connecticut, and from there Emott rode on horseback a good sixty-five miles to Boston arriving late in the evening of Tuesday, June 13, 1699, three days after he'd received Kidd's letter. He made his way to the stately home of Peter Sergeant, a wealthy merchant who owned one of the finest homes in downtown Boston on Marlborough Street facing the Old South Church. Built in 1679, it was a three-story square brick mansion with a cupola on the top. Sergeant had given the house over to the new governor for his use. The governor's council met in one of the best chambers. (The brick structure was later known as Province House—and a plaque today says "The Home of the Provincial Governors.")[1]

Lord Bellomont suffered from chronic bouts of gout, a painful disease that manifested itself in his feet. On the night of Emott's visit, Bellomont received him in the library, likely with his leg propped up on a footstool and in some discomfort. He welcomed Emott graciously, or graciously enough for someone who later wrote to the Council of Trade and Plantations that he was "a little pussiled [puzzled] how to manage Emot, a cunning Jacobite, a fast Friend of [Governor] Fletcher's and my avowed enemy."[2] Despite his personal dislike of Emott, Lord Bellomont heard him out. Kidd's letter appealed to the governor, as his investor and business partner, to support and protect him against charges of piracy. Kidd vehemently denied that he was a pirate, and he supplied as proof two French Passes he obtained from ships he captured in the Indian Ocean. Emott informed Lord Bellomont that Kidd had a great deal of treasure with him, including sixty pounds weight of gold, about one hundred weight of silver, and seventeen bales of East India goods with a total value of £10,000.[3] And there was more on a ship hidden in Hispaniola in the West Indies with a value of about £30,000.[4]

Only Kidd knew where the vessel was hidden. If Lord Bellomont would grant Kidd a pardon and indemnity against loss on the £20,000 bond he gave as his share of the investment in the voyage (the one Livingston had to back up and Kidd gave Livingston as collateral for the property he owned at 86-90 Pearl Street), Kidd would turn over the valuable cargo he had and retrieve the treasure-laden ship in Hispaniola.[5]

While Captain Kidd waited for Emott to return with an answer from Lord Bellomont, he masterminded another plan to safeguard his family. From Stonington, Connecticut, he sailed up to Jamestown, Rhode Island (near Newport), and left a significant amount of gold with his friend Captain Thomas Paine, a sixty-seven-year-old ex-pirate. Kidd asked Paine to protect the gold and dispense it through a messenger when Sarah needed money. He then sailed to Block Island and, pulling in close to the shore, unloaded two 300-pound cannon and a stockpile of ammunition on the front lawn of Captain Edward Sands's home, knowing that Sarah would be staying there and might need protection.[6] After dropping the cannon, Kidd hovered at the agreed-upon spot three leagues (about nine miles) from Block Island.

On Saturday, June 17, 1699, four days after his meeting with Bellomont, Emott returned, accompanied by Duncan Campbell, a former bookseller and now Boston's postmaster. Campbell was a Scotsman like Captain Kidd and an old acquaintance. It was pure coincidence that he had now been tasked with delivering to Kidd important communication from the governor. Emott and Campbell, still wearing wigs, waistcoats, and buckle shoes, were tired from the two-day trip from Boston but Campbell delivered Bellomont's encouraging greeting. The governor invited Captain Kidd to Boston and assured him that a pardon was possible. Kidd decided the verbal communication was too vague. He wanted something in writing—a response in-kind. He dispatched Campbell back to Boston to get the promise in writing and sent with him a gift of an enameled box with four jewels in it for Countess Kate Bellomont.[7] The gift was a sign of goodwill. Countess Kate Bellomont showed the generous present to her husband and Bellomont advised her to keep it "lest it might offend Kidd and prevent a true development."[8]

Kidd was getting antsy so he cruised twenty-seven miles west to Gardiner's Island, a remote island near the mouth of Long Island Sound. The 3,300-acre wooded estate was known to mariners for its private location and the warm hospitality of its owner, John Gardiner, the third lord of the manor. Gardiner lived on the isolated island with his wife, some farmhands, a few Indigenous people, horses, pigs, sheep, rare birds, and plenty of fish and shellfish. The island paradise was a perfect place for Captain Kidd to "grocery shop" for provisions and ask the proprietor for a couple of favors.

Emott must have believed that Captain Kidd was assured of a pardon and that his work as a go-between was complete because he asked John Gardiner for a boat to take him back to New York.[9] He'd been gone about a week and he had his family, church duties, and law practice to get back to.

Kidd asked Gardiner to look after his "four young Negro slaves"—three boys and a girl—that he had brought with him from Madagascar and two bales of goods.[10] He also asked for six sheep and a barrel of hard cider for his reunion feast with Sarah.[11] Gardiner agreed to help. He later reported that he did not know Kidd was a pirate but that even if he did know, "he durst not have acted otherwise, having no force to oppose, and he hath formerly been threatened to be killed by Privateers, if he should carry unkindly" to them.[12] After an offer of payment for the sheep and cider, Kidd gave Mrs. Gardiner a gratitude gift of a pitcher and a piece of woven silk cloth embroidered in gold thread. Kidd told Mrs. Gardiner that he took it from his legitimate prize sailing under a French Pass, the Moorish ship the *Quedah Merchant*, and that it was part of the wedding trousseau of the Great Mogul's daughter.[13] Then he sailed off toward the rendezvous point to meet Campbell, firing a four-gun salute of thanks to the Gardiners as he left.[14]

13

Safe Haven on Block Island

After a several-hour journey from Manhattan, Thomas Clark notified Sarah that they were approaching land. Sarah, the girls, and Elizabeth Morris waited as the boat was steered into the deep-water harbor on the southeastern side of Block Island. The crossing from Manhattan to Block Island was more than just exhausting, it was transformative for Sarah. In Manhattan, she was a New York socialite married to a successful and respected privateer. On Block Island, she was the wife of an accused pirate and an accomplice to a man on the run from the law. If Sarah had not realized the seriousness of the situation, she certainly must have understood when she saw the two cannon and a large stash of ammunition that Kidd had left for her protection on the front lawn of the home of her friends, Mary and Edward Sands.[1] The cannon pointing toward the harbor sent a clear message.

As she greeted Sarah, Mary may have been wearing the only pair of shoes she owned. Her homemade ankle-length frock was, as one Block Island resident described it, "pale of the blandishments and corruptions of fashion."[2] Sarah's

high-fashion clothes, complete with accessories and matching
shoes, did not fit in on Block Island. But the familiar faces
along her journey must have provided some comfort. Her
husband had orchestrated her safe passage by relying on his
network of close friends and confidants. First James Emott,
then Thomas Clark, and now Edward and Mary Sands. She
was safe for the moment.

The pear-shaped Block Island, just three miles wide, seven
miles long, and thirteen miles from the southern coast of
Rhode Island, was a world unto its own with its own economy, militia, and system of governance. Mary's family had
been connected with some of the leading smugglers, money
launderers, and black marketers in New England for generations.[3] And there were a lot of such people passing through
the island.[4]

Illegal activity on Block Island was originally a means to
an end, a way for islanders to survive the severe trade restrictions the British imposed on the colonies. On Block Island,
the cash shortage was so dire that residents bartered pork,
beef, wheat, barley, butter, tallow, and cheese as legal tender.[5]

Pirates and smugglers, with their stolen goods and gold
and silver coins, offered tangible relief to the depressed Block
Island economy. The island garnered a reputation among
mariners as a "receptacle" of pirates' goods and its residents
provided a safe harbor for miscreants.[6] Plus, the secluded
deep-water harbor made it ideal for ships to come and go un-
noticed. Mary's own brother, Captain Paulsgrave Williams,
was himself a pirate. He returned to Block Island in 1717 to
see his mother and three sisters and unload some of the loot

he and his piratical partner Samuel Bellamy captured from over fifty ships.

From the Sandses' home, Sarah most likely would have seen and heard about illegal cargo loaded and unloaded from ships in the harbor. Edward Sands had recently inherited the family homestead from his late father. It was a center of the community, "the hospitable home for visitors, a place of worship for the Islanders and a hospital for the poor and suffering," as one local described it.[7] Situated on four hundred acres near the harbor, the Sandses' home was a self-contained world with horses, sheep, pigs, cattle, several enslaved workers, a millpond, and a mill.[8] Edward's mother, Sarah Sands, was not only the matriarch of the large Sands family, but also the island's only midwife and doctor. One of the jobs of a colonial midwife was to ask the mother, usually during the height of labor and at her most vulnerable, who fathered the child. This process of identifying paternity was so important to the Block Island community that Sarah Sands was required to testify under oath that the information she reported to the town clerk was true and accurate.[9] Her sworn statement was entered into the Town Record Book. Sarah Sands's skills as a midwife and her credibility made her one of the most important women in the community. The authorities would soon question her about her houseguest, who arrived on short notice.

14

Reunited

Captain Kidd anchored off the east end of Block Island and readied for the reunion with his wife and children. Wanting to look his best for Sarah, he put on his waistcoat with nine diamond buttons[1] and new shoulder-length brown wig that Emott picked up for him in Boston. (Beyond defending him against piracy charges, Emott was also Kidd's personal shopper, selecting the handsome wig from among the many styles of the day for the price of four pistoles of gold.)[2] Kidd asked his men to prepare the lamb and season it with the cloves and nutmeg he had on hand.[3] The small crew of thirteen men[4] set out the pewter tankards and opened the barrel of cider supplied by John Gardiner. Kidd sent a small boat ashore to fetch his family and friends while he stayed on board to guard the treasure.

Sarah prepared for the reunion by changing into one of her New York Sunday best. The girls, too, would have been in pretty floor-length dresses to impress their father.

Sarah stepped from the small boat onto the deck of the *Saint Antonio*. Steadying herself with a hard grasp of the railing, she took in the sight of the man in front of her. Kidd had sailed halfway around the world and back; through him she saw the interconnectedness of the world. Now forty-five-years-old, Kidd may have looked different to her, not just from the wear and tear of life at sea, but because of the experience of going from a respected man to an accused pirate. Noticeably missing from among the crew members was Samuel Jr., her brother. Sarah asked where he was and Captain Kidd had to explain that he had been very sick throughout most of the voyage with an illness that may have been a virulent dysentery.[5] Weak and in pain, Samuel begged his brother-in-law to put him onshore so that he could seek care. Kidd hesitated to let him go, knowing Sarah would be very upset that he'd left Samuel behind. But after much insistence, Kidd granted Samuel his wishes and allowed him to go ashore in St. Thomas where the five men who carried him then deserted.[6] Sarah knew it could not have been an easy decision especially because her husband was so fond of Samuel. And Samuel looked up to Kidd as a mentor, so much so, he named him in his will.[7] She knew, though, that her brother could be very insistent and she was relieved Kidd allowed him to get medical care. Samuel would likely write to them from St. Thomas and return to New York when he was able.

Duncan Campbell, the fellow Scotsman, had returned to the ship with a letter from Lord Bellomont and was waiting for Captain Kidd's response. In private, Kidd discussed Lord Bellomont's letter with Sarah. Sarah was a savvy woman. From the loss of her mother and two husbands she had developed strong survival instincts. Captain Kidd wanted—and needed—to hear his wife's gut reaction. Three years apart did not diminish his trust and confidence in her. The governor summarized the details of his meeting with Emott and encouraged Captain Kidd by saying "if your case be so clear as you (or Mr. Emott for you) have said, you may safely come hither…and I make no manner of doubt but to obtain the King's pardon for you."[8]

The Kidds wanted to believe him. If he was found innocent of piracy, a good share of Kidd's treasure would go to Bellomont, and he could finally stop complaining to the Board of Trade about their slow reimbursement of the business expenses he paid out of pocket to keep the New York province running. But something about Bellomont's wording caught their attention; it was the conditional phrase "If your case be so clear as you have said…" Maybe that was just the governor's writing style—he was a prolific letter writer jotting off hundreds of lengthy dispatches since he took office. Or maybe he was distracted from the pain of his gout and hastily wrote Captain Kidd knowing that their relationship was not as formal as with others.

But this was a life-or-death situation. If Kidd was found guilty of piracy he would face a public hanging, not unlike Leisler and Milborne. Kidd lifted the lid of his sea trunk where he kept his ink pot and quill. When his crew had mutinied in Madagascar they ransacked the trunk, stole his gold, and destroyed his journal—his only written record of the voyage.[9] They also took "a great many papers that belonged to him and the People of New-York that fitted them out."[10] The two French Passes, however, weren't stolen. They were proof that he had captured the French ships and cargo lawfully. Sarah welcomed that news. It was *the* evidence that proved her husband was not a pirate.

But in Kidd's mind, he was grappling with another story; the truth of what really happened on his voyage. He had also pursued non-French ships. Under great pressure from his crew, he succumbed to the temptation of capturing several prizes on the coast of Malabar that were not within the terms of his letter of marque. Sometimes Kidd was a privateer, and at other times, he was a pirate. He was neither all good nor all bad, but a mix of both.

It was not unusual for privateering to readily pass into piracy. Once out at sea, the crew and captain realized that sharing the profits of a treasure with investors was bad for business, especially when they had been at sea for several years—as Kidd had been—without capturing a prize. The terms of Kidd's agreement with his crew, "no prey—no pay" meant they did not get paid if they did not capture a prize, and for too long they had not taken a ship. Kidd and his men were depressed, sick, hungry, and poor. Something had to change and it meant that Kidd, as captain, had to be more flexible.

It was Kidd's galling actions against East India ships that brought him to the attention of the authorities. In August 1697 he attacked one of their ships but was driven away. In November 1697 he made another attempt, but failed. The East India Company demanded that the British government brand Kidd a pirate. Letters were sent to every governor notifying them that Captain Kidd was a pirate and was on the loose. He was the most wanted man on the planet.

Kidd had to explain to Sarah how he came to have a ship

full of treasure. And that there was another one in Hispaniola, the *Quedah Merchant* (that he renamed the *Adventure Prize*) that he hid in a creek tied to a tree in the River Higuey.[11] A merchant named Henry Bolton was keeping watch over it and he left eighteen of his men to safeguard the valuable cargo.[12] He had to share with her why time was of the essence and why he needed her help to get out of this dangerous situation.

His explanation, a confession of sorts, must have been terrifying for her. At the time she married Kidd, he was one of the most respected men in New York. He was her hero and the father of her children. The enormity of the situation could only begin to sink in. Sarah had seen pirates walking the streets of New York for as long as she lived there. She saw their ships in the harbor—welcome visitors under Governor Fletcher—and their active trade with local merchants selling their exotic goods at bargain prices. But it is doubtful that Sarah had ever been aboard a pirate ship or knew the men who strutted in their stolen finery on the docks of Manhattan.

15

Accomplice

Sarah was now an insider in that much-talked-about fraternity of sea robbers. She had an up close and very personal glimpse into the rough life aboard a pirate ship. On board the vessel—a timbered hull with ropes, fittings, and sails—was a small ragtag group of salty unwashed men that included a murderous pirate from Madagascar, James Gilliam, who had slit the throat of a sleeping merchant captain.[1] The ship smelled of salty sea air, damp perspiration, mildew, and bad breath. The latrine was a bucket or a hole in a plank unceremoniously positioned off the side of the ship. Sarah was among the cannon and gun shot, pistols and swords. She walked past so much stolen loot—gold and silver coins, jewels, drugs, spices, and textiles tied into bales. It had taken years of hard work for Kidd to make "payroll" so that the men would have something to show for their time away from their families. The *Saint Antonio* rode low in the water with the weight of all Kidd's precious cargo—his family, friends, and chests of gold. For Sarah, it was a far cry from life in her Pearl Street mansion with its tieback curtains and feather beds.

★ ★ ★

At the top of the letter, Kidd wrote in his perfect handwriting, "From Block Island Road [Rhode Island], On Board the Sloop St. Antonio." The date was Saturday, June 24, 1699. It had been exactly two weeks since Emott came to Sarah's house and turned her life upside down. Kidd dipped his quill in the pot of ink and turned the paper over as he wrote more, defending himself against the "clamorous and false stories" that had been reported about him.[2] He reiterated that he did not act contrary to the king's commission, and that he took great care to preserve the owners' interests. He had come "to these parts of the world" to prove his "innocency."[3] He thanked Bellomont for his encouraging letter of support and said he would make his way to Boston without delay. He signed it "My Lord, Your Excellency's Most humble and dutyfull Servant, Wm. Kidd."[4]

Sarah quickly changed out of her Sunday best. There was work to do and she only had a little while to wrap her mind around what could come next. Kidd needed Sarah to do more than fold his waistcoat and tuck it safely in his trunk, as she did three years ago when he prepared for his privateering voyage. Kidd wanted—and needed—Sarah to be his co-captain. As a pirate's wife, she was now his extra pair of eyes and ears operating on high alert. It was a position she embraced.

Captain Kidd ordered the anchor raised. A small boat pulled alongside of the *Saint Antonio*. The crew, seeing Kidd give Campbell a letter sealed with his signet ring, expected to set the course eastward for Boston. The *Saint Antonio*'s sails filled. Only Sarah Sands could have seen from her vantage on

Block Island that the ship that still held her son and daughter-in-law veered west. The treasure-laden vessel was not making its way to Boston as Kidd had told Bellomont it would.

16

Buried Treasure

John Gardiner recognized the man in the small boat rowing toward him. It was the master of the *Saint Antonio* and he was signaling for Gardiner to get in. Together they rowed out to the anchored ship where Kidd was waiting. As he boarded the *Saint Antonio*, he noticed something had changed since Kidd's visit three days ago. "Captain Kidd's wife was then on board," Gardiner reported in a deposition.[1] Sarah was standing on the ship's deck next to Kidd.

Kidd told Gardiner he needed his help—again—this time to safeguard the rest of the treasure.[2] His demeanor was deadly serious. He was not the same visitor who signaled a casual maritime goodbye with cannon shots. Kidd gave Gardiner a small chest that was "nailed, corded about, and sealed." It contained his most important things: three small bags of Jasper Antonio or stone of Goa (a fever medicine consisting of various drugs made up into a hard ball by the Jesuits of Goa), several pieces of silk with silver and gold stripes, spices—including a bushel of cloves and nutmegs mixed together—fine white calicoes and muslins and flowered silk.[3] He also gave him a bundle of nine or ten fine India quilts, some of them made of silk with fringes and tassels.[4] These last things he prized the most and it could be that he intended Sarah to have them at a later date. Three of Kidd's crew asked Gardiner to hold their coarse canvas bags of gold, silver, and gold dust as well as a few personal items like a sash and a pair of "worsted stockins."[5]

Kidd asked Gardiner if he could bury some treasure on his property. Gardiner pointed him in the direction of the heavily wooded forest between Bostwick's Point and the manor house. Kidd and his men rowed to the island in the small boat and found a place that was impossible for anyone to notice that the ground had been disturbed.[6] In a ravine thick with ground cover Kidd had his men dig until they had a hole large enough to bury the forty-pound chest filled with 300–400 pieces of eight valued at about $30,000.[7] A few of the gold pieces belonged to Kidd's cabin boy, Richard Barleycorn.[8] (The spot on the privately owned island where Kidd buried his treasure is now identified with a granite marker, according to a Gardiner descendant.)[9]

Sarah took an inventory of the remaining treasure. She knew what was in the bags, boxes, and chests, fastened with cords, chains, and locks. The items were some of the most fabulous riches collected from the other side of the world. Gardiner reported that he saw two chests leave Kidd's ship. It is very likely that Sarah selected the items to go in the chests which included "eleven small pearls, a skein of gold thread, a bag of ten pounds of spice, 3½ yards of silk fringe, four pounds of gold and forty pounds of silver."[10] She may have intended to retrieve them later, for the items—especially the thread and yards of silk fringe—were in keeping with her taste and much like the goods she and Cox sold in their shop. There is little doubt that Sarah packed them as carefully as she folded Kidd's waistcoat.

Gardiner said he believed several more chests were taken away in the New York sloop moored next to the *Saint Antonio*. Thomas Clark, Kidd's friend who ushered Sarah to Block Island, was on that New York sloop and he may have stashed the treasure in his secret warehouse in Stamford, Connecticut.[11]

Having a woman's touch on a pirate ship was highly unusual. Women were normally forbidden on pirate ships because it was believed they would distract the crew. The rule was so established it was included in many ship's articles. Sarah's presence as the pirate's wife and her elevated position next to Captain Kidd was unprecedented in pirate history. There have been several women pirates on pirate ships: Anne Bonny and Mary Read were among the most notable. They disguised themselves by dressing as men and when the pirate ship they were on was captured, they were tried along with their male counterparts. Bonny and Read escaped execution by "pleading the belly," meaning that they were pregnant and given a reprieve. Sarah was *not* a pirate. She did not break the law plundering merchant trading vessels. She joined Kidd after the fact which made her an accomplice to an outlaw, not an outlaw herself.

Kidd's decision to have Sarah with him meant that the crew had to mind what manners they had. The boss's wife was on board. Kidd, the tough guy with a short temper, let his guard down. His men saw that their captain didn't just navigate by the stars, he navigated by his heart and that for Kidd, home was wherever Sarah was. She was his ballast.

Sarah's willingness to join Kidd on his pirate ship put herself and her children in harm's way. She entered into a rogue's underworld guided by her love and deep trust in her husband. The evidence suggests that she believed it was important—crucial, in fact—that the girls reunite with their father, a man whose last name they shared, but who had not seen them for most of their lives.

There was no playbook for Sarah on how to be a pirate's wife. Her friends could not advise her; her mother could not support her. She was alone in a role that had no cultural norms or religious scriptures to follow. Sarah was guided by her strengths, the characteristics that Kidd celebrated—courage, commitment, and love. Those fueled her to stand tall with a man accused of murdering a crew member and committing piracy on the high seas.

The *Saint Antonio* stayed at anchor overnight and the next morning Kidd met with Gardiner again.[12] Sarah and Kidd were concerned they would not be able to find food until they reached Boston. Kidd imposed on Gardiner one more time, asking Mrs. Gardiner to prepare a pig for him.[13] Mrs. Gardiner knew that Sarah and the children were on board. It would be neighborly to feed Kidd's family. But there was another reason she cooperated with the pirate captain with a shipload of hungry men. It was the same reason Gardiner was so attentive to Kidd's requests. The blustery Kidd had threatened the life of Gardiner and his son if anything untoward happened to the treasure he was safekeeping. Kidd was not to be messed with.

The scent of a roasted pig wafted up the rigging, across the decks, down the hatchways, and into the cargo hold. It smelled like it was cooked in a gourmet chef's kitchen. Gardiner reported that Mrs. Gardiner did the pig "nicely." As a thank-you gift for all of their assistance, Kidd gave Gardiner a bag of sugar,[14] a special luxury item from the West Indies that was scarce at that time. (Kidd had on board fifty-seven more bags of sugar that were considered part of his treasure.)[15]

With the bulk of the treasure distributed, Kidd's hands were clear of it, putting him in a strong position to leverage a deal with Bellomont. If the governor wanted to know where all the treasure was hidden, including the ship in Hispaniola, he would need to come through with a pardon.

Kidd still had several young Malagasy enslaved workers, including three boys and a girl, whom Gardiner briefly looked after. Robert Livingston and Duncan Campbell each received a young male worker as a gift.[16]

Sarah was aware of how the youngsters came to be captives in the *Saint Antonio*, a ship ironically named for a saint. It was a business arrangement with the tribal leaders in Madagascar: pirate loot exchanged for enslaved people. Among the depositions given by crew members and Gardiner who noted Sarah's presence on the *Saint Antonio*, no one indicated that Sarah objected to Kidd's use of the young children as currency. If she noticed the children's hopeless expressions, or thought about the fact that they were forcibly removed from *their* mothers and fathers never to see them again, she would have winced and used her influence with Kidd to

protest his abhorrent use of children. She could have argued that breaking up a family was antithetical to what he
believed because *he insisted* on having *his* family with him.

But Sarah did not wince. Kidd trusted her and respected
her opinion but she did not use that power in their relationship to protect these innocent children. From the time Sarah
arrived in New York, she not only accepted that slavery
was a part of the culture but she benefitted greatly from it.
Moll was a tremendous help to her. Being a mother of two
did not influence her perception of the institution and the
young participants in it. She could not see that the "home"
on the *Saint Antonio* for her children was hell for the other
youngsters. She had to have been aware that her daughters
saw the Malagasy children, especially the three boys and a
girl who reboarded the *Saint Antonio* in front of them. All
of the children, Elizabeth, little Sarah, and the enslaved
children, were about the same age and maybe even around
the same height—three or four feet tall. Sarah's daughters
could look the children in the eyes and notice that while
they stayed above deck in the fresh air and bright sunlight
with their parents, the orphaned children lived in the bow-
els of the ship, the dark, damp, scary part where the chests,
boxes, and coarse canvas bags were stored. Sarah supported
Kidd's attitudes and his behavior. They were a well-matched
couple with shared values (or, when it came to slavery, lack
thereof), outlooks, and goals.

Those that saw Sarah and noted her presence as "Captain Kidd's wife" in their depositions—the Gardiners, three
crew members, and several friends and associates—all neglected to include any physical description of her. While we

do not know what Sarah looked like, we do know that during this stressful high-stakes drama she never lost her focus. She was determined to protect the well-being and future of *her* family. Marriage and motherhood were the cornerstones of her life.

The detour to Gardiner's Island took about twenty-four hours. Kidd knew that any further delay would be greeted with great suspicion by Bellomont. Bellomont knew how long it took for a skilled mariner like Kidd to sail from Block Island to Boston. Kidd and Bellomont were in a political cat and mouse game, each hedging their bets. Neither one trusted the other and they both were keeping secrets. Big secrets.

Anxious to make his way to Boston, Kidd dropped Mary and Edward Sands at Block Island. The authorities later asked Mary Sands about her visit with Sarah and Kidd. She gave the only eyewitness account about the events that took place on board the *Saint Antonio*. Mary did not betray Sarah's confidences and the native Block Islander did not reveal that she'd spent time on a ship laden with silver and gold. Mary focused instead on the passenger, James Gilliam, "the fifty-ish leather-faced, scarred old pirate who seemed very urgent to go to Rhode Island."[17] Mary kept the faith with her maritime sister, Sarah. Sarah could count her as one of her treasures.

Kidd's route to Boston took him east near Martha's Vineyard and Nantucket, around the arm of Cape Cod, then northwest into Boston Harbor. Off Nantucket, on June 30, 1699, Kidd had a serendipitous encounter with an acquaintance, Captain Thomas Way, a master mariner from Boston, who had just returned from the Bay of Campeche, in the Gulf of Mexico.[18] The two captains hailed each other and

Kidd signaled for Captain Way to come aboard.[19] Captain Way rowed over in his ship's canoe.

Kidd asked Way if he would be his guide into Boston. The shifting sandbars on the outer shores of Cape Cod, a fifty-mile stretch between Chatham and Provincetown, had caused many devastating shipwrecks. Mariners still spoke of the earliest recorded one, seventy-five years before, in 1626, with the demise of the *Sparrow-hawk*, a small boat loaded with colonists on their way to the Jamestown Colony in Virginia.[20] As a local mariner well aware of the Cape's reputation as the "ocean's graveyard," Captain Way knew how to safely navigate the terrain of the arm-shaped peninsula and wind his way through the dozens of harbor islands to the entrance to Boston's natural deep-water harbor.

Kidd and Sarah hatched a last-minute plan that put to the test Captain Way's interest in helping a fellow mariner. They wanted Way to smuggle into Boston a secret stash of goods, a pirate's wife survival kit. Kidd wanted to make sure Sarah would be safe, comfortable, and able to "pay her charges"[21] if the *Saint Antonio* was seized and/or if anything happened to him. The request was a big ask. If Captain Way was caught sneaking around Boston with a parcel that belonged to Kidd, he could be dragged into the ugly political quagmire and questioned by the authorities for his role as an accessory to an outlaw. Sensing some hesitation, Kidd gave Captain Way a "bit of a bar of gold" to warm his enthusiasm.[22]

Captain Way returned to his ship with the pirate's wife survival kit. He made sure the small bundle of Sarah's clothes, a six-pound bag of her New York money, a balance scale to weigh gold, a turkey work carpet, a pendulum navigation clock, and three flintlock pistols were stored in a safe, dry place.[23] Kidd gave him specific instructions to deliver some of the goods to Duncan Campbell's house where they would be staying and to keep the other items hidden in his Boston home until further notice.

Sarah and Kidd had taken every precaution they could think of except one. There was still time to abort the trip to Boston, dig up the buried treasure on Gardiner's Island, and retrieve other troves of treasure left in friendly hands along Long Island Sound, including at Tarpaulin Cove.[24] With the help of Kidd's vast network of friends and colleagues from many years of privateering, he and Sarah could escape to the Caribbean Islands where, now that there was peace with France, they could live comfortably and quietly.

But Kidd believed he could convince Bellomont of his innocence and clear his name. The offer of a pardon excited Kidd to imagine a life of freedom with Sarah. No more anxiety and fearing for his life as he had since April 1698 when he was accused of turning pirate. Kidd's denial that he was a pirate was, in part, because many a privateer's sojourn into piracy was overlooked, or at least winked at, by some men in authority.[25] Reminding Bellomont that he, and only he, knew where he left the treasure ship in Hispaniola would help facilitate the discussion, Kidd believed. Saving face was important to Kidd not only for himself, but for Sarah. He did not want her to suffer the harsh stigma and consequences associated with being a pirate's wife.[26]

Kidd readied his sails and waited for Captain Way's signal.

17

Confronting Bellomont

Bellomont's soldiers at the waterfront were the first to see the *Saint Antonio* sail into Boston harbor on a blistering hot Saturday, July 1, 1699. Bellomont was notified immediately, but he did not meet Kidd at the dock. He didn't want to be seen in public with him. Instead he sent a greeting and ordered that refreshments—probably cold drinks to satisfy their thirst from the heat—be sent to all of those aboard the *Saint Antonio*. The gesture was meant to convey to Kidd that Bellomont was his friend and ally, but really it was a bogus political move to lure Kidd and his crew off the *Saint Antonio* and into Boston where he had plans for them. Sarah may have been leery of the reception and felt vulnerable. They had made the trip to Boston with their fingers crossed that Bellomont was a man of his word. By not gracing them with his appearance he gave the clear impression he was too busy to make time for them. His letters had been welcoming; they expected to see him at the dock. Standing close to Kidd and her children, Sarah may have been keenly aware of the optics of the moment—Captain and Mrs. William Kidd and their children arrived in Boston on a pirate ship.

Several members of the crew loaded the Kidds' trunks into a small boat and rowed Kidd, his family, Elizabeth Morris, and the enslaved Malagasy workers to shore; then returned to the ship to stand guard. It was the first time in three years Sarah and Kidd had been on land together. This occasion marked another milestone for Kidd: from the time he left New York in the summer of 1695, to his return to Boston, he had sailed an estimated distance of forty-two thousand miles in four vessels.[1] They walked the narrow, crooked streets of Boston to the North End where Duncan Campbell and his well-to-do young heiress wife, Susannah, offered them lodging in their fine home. In gratitude for their hospitality, Kidd gave Mrs. Campbell "a gold chain, a piece of India silk, and three pieces of muslin."[2] Duncan Campbell received an enslaved worker, some cloth, and a promise of £500 if he helped Kidd win a pardon.[3] Their son, Matthew, received Kidd's walking cane—a fashion accessory—and a ten-pound box of candy.[4]

Kidd was anxious to meet with Bellomont to plead his case and secure a pardon. He requested an immediate appointment, but Bellomont insisted they meet with witnesses present. He was hired by the king to rid the colony of pirates, he told several people privately, and being seen with Kidd one-on-one could tarnish his reputation, he feared.[5]

While Kidd waited for Bellomont, he and Sarah, as ordinary visitors in this Puritan town of about fifteen hundred families,[6] attended church. They likely visited King's Chapel, the small wooden Anglican church and the first of its kind in New England, located on the corner of Tremont and School Street. Sarah and Kidd sat in the visitors' section in the back or in the second-floor gallery overlooking the congregation. What they saw was a sea of colors: boxed pews housed the paying congregants who decorated their small "rooms" with chairs and benches upholstered in red, blue, or green fabric. Sarah, as we know, was deeply religious. Attending church immediately upon arriving in Boston suggests her strong need to resume her prayerful ritual, especially after spending several days on a pirate ship.

To pass the time until Bellomont granted him an appointment, Kidd frequented the Blue Anchor Tavern, a popular meeting place to eat, drink, and take in gossip.[7] After three years at sea, it must've felt good to rub elbows with the locals and the mariners, many of whom were in between trading voyages. Hearing the latest news and rumors was important intelligence for Kidd, who may not have known the extent to which he was a wanted man.

The long weekend over, on Monday, July 3, at five o'clock in the evening, Kidd was asked to appear before Bellomont and the governor's ten-member council to give an account of his three-year voyage. The meeting took place at Bellomont's residence. The minutes of the council read:[8]

Captain William Kidd, by command of his Excellency and Council this day at five o'clock, post meridiem, to give an account of his proceedings in his late voyage to Madagascar, the said Kidd accordingly appeared, and prayed his Lordship to allow him some time and he would prepare an account in writing of his proceedings, and present to his Lordship and the Board. Time was granted him to prepare and bring in his narrative until to-marrow at five o'clock, post meridiem, as also an invoice of the bill of lading on board the sloop and the ship, attested to by himself and some of his principal officers, with a list of the names of the men on board the sloop and ship, and of those who belonged to the Adventure Galley, who, he alleges, refused to obey his commands, and evil entreated him and deserted the said ship. And the Council adjourned unto the said day and hour, after Captain Kidd had given a summary account of the lading on board his sloop now in port and also on board the ship left at Hispaniola. His Excellency appointed Captain Hawes, Deputy-Collector, to put some waiters on board.

Kidd was asked to give a full accounting of his goods. He listed bales of calicoes, silks, and muslins; tons of sugar, iron, and saltpeter; anchors; fifty cannon; eighty pounds of silver, and a forty-pound bag of gold.[9] He gave the names of the men that refused to obey him and who, he claimed, did "evil entreated him and deserted the ship."[10] Kidd testified that his journal had been violently destroyed by his crew at Saint Marie in Madagascar but if granted the time, he would prepare a narrative in writing and give a complete account of his activities.[11] Bellomont and the council agreed to give Kidd twenty-four hours to write his narrative.

Kidd went to the meeting thinking that if he appeared in person, wearing his dress coat and new wig Duncan Campbell purchased for him, he could convince Bellomont of his innocence and Bellomont would quickly issue him a pardon. The demand for a written account put him on the spot. A public statement could be fact-checked. There were many written complaints made about Kidd, especially by the East India Company. The dossier on him was thick.

Kidd may have stopped at the Blue Anchor Tavern for a drink before returning to Duncan Campbell's house to put pen to paper. On the walk back to the North End he had time to think and compose the words that would appease Bellomont and his council. The stern wigged men wanted to know every detail starting from when he left London under the banner of a privateer with two mighty letters of marque.

No doubt he consulted Sarah who was waiting for him to return and asked her advice like he did on the *Saint Antonio* when he crafted his first reply to Bellomont. If Kidd had not already shared with Sarah all the details of his voyage, he likely did now. He needed her help and support; he was up against the authorities and this was serious business. They discussed a strategy of what to do and say. Sarah must have felt a flood of emotions as she looked at Kidd and listened. They may have run the gamut from anger at Kidd for getting himself (and her) into this situation, to compassion for the man who believed he was betrayed by his mutinous crew. Apart from her feelings as a wife, she must've also been thinking of her brother, Samuel Jr., who witnessed brutal violence and learned firsthand why pirates are considered the "enemy of all mankind." The hard-core rogues had no allegiance to anyone or any country, only to themselves for their own gain.

The narrative was an onerous assignment. Kidd would have to relive in his mind every hour, day, week, month, and year for three years. He started to remember bits and pieces…the disease, death of his crewmen, shortage of naval supplies, the need for food and water; the angry crew, his disciplinary actions, the loud boom of cannon fire; men fighting, villagers screaming, and the rage and tears from women who had been raped. Kidd had three long difficult years to account for, but there were events he could not include. He had to hope that his word would stand up against those intending to incriminate him. After all, he was chosen for the job because of his stellar credentials and the most powerful men in England believed he was the right man for the job. The loss of his journal gave Kidd a reason to "forget" some damning episodes. Creating a new narrative would take time. Each word had to be carefully chosen. By the allotted time on Tuesday, July 4, the narrative was not complete. Twenty-four hours had not been enough.

The details of his voyage started to come flooding back. He may have closed his eyes as he remembered what really happened.

18

Kidd's Narrative

With the story fresh in his head, Kidd began to write. Dipping the quill pen into a pot of black ink, he touched the flattened parchment and wrote the first words: "A Narrative of the Voyage of Captain William Kidd, Commander of the *Adventure Gally*, from London to the East Indies…"

Kidd appeared before Bellomont the next day, Tuesday, July 4, 1699, with five of his crewmen who presented their written affidavits relating to Kidd's voyage. Kidd had not completed his own affidavit and Bellomont wanted to read Kidd's own account. He gave him an extension until 5:00 p.m. the next day.

Kidd appeared the next day and still he had not finished. He was called to appear two more times. Finally he turned in his narrative.[1] Bellomont was incensed at what he considered Kidd's insolence in failing to produce his narrative in the assigned timeframe. Why Kidd took so long to write his narrative is unclear. It is possible he relayed the facts to Sarah as he wrote and she, a street-savvy woman with keen instincts, may have encouraged him to buy himself more time. They employed this strategy with Bellomont before while on the *Saint Antonio*. It is safe to say that Sarah had a significant part in helping Kidd formulate a narrative that painted him in a favorable light as an innocent man who was a victim of his circumstances—a mutinous crew and bad luck.

Kidd's (and Sarah's) telling of the voyage is contrary to many of the reports in the primary sources. He omitted events where he made untruthful statements—for example, when he lied to four captains of East India Company ships telling them he was going to Saint Marie to capture pirates when he fully intended to go to the Red Sea and plunder the pilgrim fleet, saying to his crew, "Come, boys, I will make money enough out of that fleet," his crewman, Joseph Palmer, reported at Kidd's trial.[2]

He never admitted to the stopover at the Laccadive Islands where his crew unleashed a flurry of violence against the locals, burning their boats and raping a number of the native women. He did not mention the fact that his cooper's neck was slit as a result of his crew's atrocious behavior or that he captured an escaping villager, tied him to a tree, and ordered the man to be shot. Instead he claimed that he went to Saint Marie to refit the failing *Adventure Galley*. Kidd was caught in this lie because the islanders reported the incident to the authorities on the mainland. He also attacked East India Company ships, an ironic and ignoble thing to do given that one of his investors, Sir Edward Harrison, was the director of the East India Company.

Kidd led people to believe that he only flew the flags of

a privateer when in fact Edward Barlow, the captain of the *Spectre*, one of the European escorts flying the flag of the East India Company, saw Kidd close to the convoy and reported in his journal, and to the East India Company, that Kidd was flying a bloodred banner that indicated they were pirates. Pirates often flew a warning flag signaling the prey to surrender, or else. The Jolly Roger, or black flag, was the most popular, but the more feared was a plain red flag which signaled death to all who saw it. If Barlow's story is true, it is highly unlikely that Kidd began the voyage with a bloodred flag in his collection of flags that he used as a ruse. Having a bloodred flag at the onset would have meant he'd intended to turn pirate from the start of his voyage, and there is no evidence to support that. If there was such a flag, the men likely made it on board from red cloth. All these details slipped Kidd's mind.

Kidd's narrative is a critical piece of evidence that sheds light on Sarah as a pirate's wife. We witness their collaborative effort to save his life and their future together. While Kidd and Sarah labored for six days, Duncan Campbell may have listened through the door and reported back to Bellomont what he heard. Bellomont wanted the postmaster to deliver any news about Kidd and Sarah. Campbell was a loyal employee of the governor.

Bellomont read Kidd's narrative, likely with his leg propped up on a footstool to relieve the pain from his gout. As he read, he may have heard in his mind the narrator's Scottish accent. The following is Kidd's (and Sarah's) account:[3]

Narrative of the Voyage of Captain William Kidd, Commander of the *Adventure Gally*, from London to the East Indies. July 7, 1699.

That the Journal of the said Captain Kidd being violently taken from him in the Port of St. Marie's in Madagascar, and his life many time being threatened to be taken away from him by 97 of his men that deserted him there, he cannot give that exact Account he otherwise could have done, but as far as his memory will serve is as followeth...:

That the said *Adventure Gally* was launched in Castle's Yard at Deptford about the 4th day of December 1695, and about the latter end of February the said galley came to the buoy in the Nore, and about the first Day of March following, his men were pressed from him for the Fleet, which caused him to stay there 19 Days, and then sailed for the Downs, and arrived there about the 8th or 10th Day of April 1696; and sailed thence for Plymouth, and on the 23d Day of the said month of April he sailed from Plymouth on his intended Voyage, and some time in the month of May met with a small French Vessel with Salt and Fishing Tackle on board, bound for Newfoundland, which he took and made Prize of and carried the same into New-York, about the 4th day of July, where she was condemned as lawful Prize, the produce whereof purchased Provisions for the said Gally for her further intended voyage.

That, about the 6th day of September 1696 the said Captain Kidd sailed for the Maderas in Company with one Joyner, Master of a Brigateen belonging to Bermudas, and arrived there about the 8th day of October following; and thence to Bonavista, where they arrived about the 19th of said month, and took in some Salt and stayed three or four days, and sailed thence to St. Jago and arrived there the 24th of the said month, where he took in some Water and staied about 8 or 9 Days, and thence sailed for the Cape of Good Hope, and in the Latitude of 32, on the 12th day of December 1696 met with four English Men of War, whereof Captain Warren was Commodore, and sailed a week in their Company, and then parted and sailed to Telere, a Port in the Island of Madagascar, and being there about the 29th day of January, came in a Sloop belonging to Barbadoes, loaded with Rhum, Sugar, Powder and Shot, one—French Master, and Mr. Hatton and Mr. John Batt Merchants, and the said Hatton came on board the said Gally and was suddenly taken ill there and dyed in the Cabin: and about the latter end of February sayled for the Island of Johanna, the said Sloop keeping Company, and arrived there about the 18th day of March, where he found Four East India Merchantmen, outward bound, and watered there all together, and stayd about four days, And from thence about the 22d of March sayled for Mehila, an Island Ten Leagues distant from Johanna, where he arrived the next morning, and there careened the said Gally, and about fifty men died there in a weekes time.

That on the 25th day of April 1697 set saile for the Coast of India, and came upon the Coast of Mallabar in the beginning of the month of September, and went into Carrwarr upon that Coast about the middle of the same month and watered there, and the Gentlemen of the English Factory gave the Narrator an Account that the Portugese were fitting out two men of War to take him, and advised him to set out to Sea, and to take care of himself from them, and immediately he set sail thereupon…about the 22d of the

said month of September, and the next morning about
break of day saw the said two Men of War standing for the
said Gally, and spoke with him, and asked him Whence he
was, who replyed, from London, and they returned answer,
from Goa, and so parted, wishing each other a good Voyage, and making still along the Coast, the Commodore of
the said Men of War kept dogging the said Gally all Night,
waiting an Opportunity to board the same, and in the
morning, without speaking a word, fired 6 great Guns at
the Gally, some whereof went through her, and wounded
four of his men, and thereupon he fired upon him again,
the Fight continued all day, and the Narrator had eleven
men wounded: The other Portuguese Men of War lay some
distance off, and could not come up with the Gally, being
calm, else would have likewise assaulted the same. The
said Fight was sharp, and the said Portuguese left the said
Gally with such Satisfaction that the Narrator believes no
Portuguese will ever attack the Kings Colours again, in
that part of the World especially, and afterwards continued
upon the said Coast, cruising upon the Cape of Cameroone
for Pyrates that frequent that Coast, till the beginning of
the month of November 1697 when he met with Captain
How in the *Loyal Capitaine*, an English Ship belonging to
Maddarass, bound to Surat, whom he examined and, finding his Pass good, designed freely to let her pass about her
affairs; but having two Dutchmen on board, they told the
narrator's men that they had divers Greeks and Armenians
on board, who had divers precious Stones and other rich
Goods on board, which caused his men to be very mutinous, and got up their Armes, and swore they would take
the Ship, and two-thirds of his Men voted for the same.
The narrator told them The small Armes belonged to the

Gally, and that he was not come to take any Englishmen or lawful Traders, and that if they attempted any such thing they should never come on board the Gally again, nor have the Boat, or Small-Armes, for he had no commission to take any but the King's Enemies, and Pirates, and that he would attack them with the Gally and drive them into Bombay; the other being a Merchantman and having no Guns, might easily have done it with a few hands, and with all the arguments and menaces he could use could scarce restraine them for their unlawful Designe, but at last prevailed, and with much ado got him clear, and let him go about his business. All which Captain How will attest, if living.

And that about the 18th or 19th day of the said month of November met with a Moors Ship of about 200 Tuns, coming from Suratt, bound to the Coast of Mallabar, loaded with two horses, Sugar and Cotton, to trade there, having about 40 Moors on board, with a Dutch Pylot, Boatswain and Gunner, which said Ship the Narrator hailed, and commanded on board, and with him came 8 or 9 Moors and the said three Dutchmen, who declared it was a Moors Ship, and demanding their Pass from Suratt, which they shewed, and the same was a French Pass, which he believes was shewed, and the same was a French Pass, which he believes was shewed by a Mistake, for the Pylot swore Sacrament she was a Prize, and staid on board the Gally and would not return again on board the Moors Ship, but went in the Gally to the Port of St. Maries.

And that about the First Day of February following, upon the same Coast, under French Colours with a Designe to decoy, met with a Bengall Merchantman belonging to Surrat of the burthen of 4 or 500 Tuns, 10 guns, and he com-

manded the Master on board, and a Frenchman, Inhabitant
of Suratt and belonging to the French Factory there, and
Gunner of said Ship, came on board as Master, and when
he came on board the Narrator caused the English Colours
to be hoisted, and the said Master was surprized and said,
You are all English; and asking, Which was the Captain,
whom when he saw, said, Here is a good Prize, and delivered him the French Pass. And that with the said two
Prizes sailed for the Port of St. Maries, in Madagascar; and
sailing thither the said Gally was so leaky that they feared
she would have sunk every hour, and it required eight
men, every two Glasses to keep her free, and was forced
to woold her round with Cables to keep her together, and
with much ado carried her into the said Port of St. Maries,
where they arrived about the First Day of April 1698, and
about the 6th day of May the lesser Prize was haled into
the Careening Island or Key, the other not being arrived,
and ransacked and sunk by the mutinous men, who threatened the Narrator and the men that would not join with
them, to burn and sink the other, that they might not go
home and tell the news.

And that when he arrived in the said Port there was a
Pyrate Ship, called the *Moca* Frigat, at an Anchor, Robert
Culliford Commander thereof, who with his men left the
same at his coming in, and ran into the Woods, And the
Narrator proposed to his men to take the same, having
sufficient power and authority so to do, but the mutinous
Crew told him, if he offered the same, they would rather
fire two Guns into him than one into the other, and thereupon 97 deserted, and went into the *Moca* Frigat, and sent
into the Woods for the said Pyrates and brought the said
Culliford and his men on board again; and all the time

she staid in the said Port, which was for the Space of 4 or 5 Dayes, the said Deserters, sometimes in great numbers, came on board the said Gally and *Adventure Prize*, and carried away great guns, Powder, Shot, small Armes, Sailes, Anchors, Cables, Chirurgeons Chest, and what else they pleased, and threatned several times to murder the Narrator (as he was informed, and advised to take care of himselfe) which they designed in the Night to effect but was prevented by his locking himselfe in his Cabin at night, and securing himselfe with barrocading the same with bales of Goods, and having about 40 small Armes, besides Pistols, ready charged, kept them out. Their wickedness was so great, after they had plundered and ransacked sufficiently, went four miles off to one Edward Welche's house, where his the Narrator's Chest was lodged, and broke it open, and took out 10 ounces of Gold, forty Pounds of Plate, 370 pieces of Eight, the Narrator's Journal, and a great many papers that belonged to him and the People of New-York that fitted them out.

That about the 15th of June, the *Moca* Frigat went away, being manned with about 130 Men and forty Guns, bound out to take all Nations. Then it was that the Narrator was left only with 13 Men, so that the Moors he had to pump and keep the *Adventure Gally* above Water being carried away, she sunk in the harbour, and the Narrator with the said thirteen men went on board of the *Adventure Prize*, where he was forced to stay five months for a fair Wind. In the meantime some Passengers presented, that were bound for these Parts, which he took on board to help bring the said *Adventure Prize* home.

That about the beginning of April 1699 the Narrator arrived at Anguilla in the West-Indies and sent his Boat on

Shore, where his men had the News That he and his People were proclaimed Pirates, which put them into such a Consternation that they sought all Opportunitys to run the Ship on shore upon some reef or Shoal, fearing the Narrator should carry them into some English port.

From Anguilla they came to St. Thomas, where his Brother-in-law Samuel Bradley was put on shore, being sick, and five more went away and deserted him, where he heard the same News, that the Narrator and his Company were proclaimed Pirates, which incensed the People more and more. From St. Thomas set saile for Moona, an Island between Hispaniola and Porto Rico, where they met with a Sloop called the *St. Anthony*, bound for Montego from Curaso, Mr. William Bolton Merchant and Samuel Wood Master. The men on board then swore they would bring the Ship no further. The Narrator then sent the said Sloop *St. Anthony* for Curaso for Canvas to make Sails for the Prize, she being not able to proceed, and she returned in 10 days, and after the Canvas came he could not persuade the men to carry her for New-England, but Six of them went and carried their Chests and things on board of two Dutch sloops, bound for Curaso, and would not so much as heele the Vessel or do any-thing; the remainder of the men not being able to bring the *Adventure Prize* to Boston, the Narrator secured her in the good safe harbor in some Part of Hispaniola, and left her in the Possession of Mr. Henry Boulton of Antego, Merchant, the Master, three of the old men, and 15 or 16 of the men that belonged to the said Sloop *St. Anthony* and a Briganteen belonging to one Burt of Curaso.

That the Narrator bought the said Sloop *St. Anthony* of Mr. Bolton, for the Owners accompt, and after he had

given Directions to the said Bolton to be careful of the Ship and Ladeing and persuaded him to stay three months till he returned, and then made the best of his way to New-York, where he heard the Earl of Bellomont was, who was principally concerned in the *Adventure Gally*, and hearing his Lordship was at Boston, came thither and has not been 45 Days from the said Ship.
Wm. Kidd

Boston, 7th July, 1699

Further the narrator saith, That the said Ship was left at St. Katharina in the Southeast part of Hispaniola, about three Leagues to Leward of the Westerly end of Savano. Whilst he lay at Hispaniola he traded with Mr. Henry Bolton of Antigua, and Mr. William Burt of Curracao, Merchants, to the value of Eleven thousand two hundred Pieces of Eight, whereof he received the Sloop Antonio at 3000 Pieces of 8/8, and four thousand two hundred Pieces of 8/8 by Bills of Exchange, drawn by Bolton and Burt upon Messieurs Gabril and Lemont, Merchants in Curracao, made payable to Mr. Burt, who went himself to Curracao, the Value of four thousand Pieces of 8/8 more in Dust and barr-gold, which Gold, with some more traded for at Madagascar, being Fifty Pound Weight and upwards in Quantity, the narrator left in Custody of Mr. Gardner of Gardner's-Island, near the Eastern end of Long-Island, fearing to bring it about by Sea. It is made up in a bagg put into a little box, lockt and nailed, corded about, and sealed. Saith, He took no receipt for it of Mr. Gardner. The Gold that was seized at Mr. Campbel's the Narrator traded for at Madagascar, with what came out of the Gally.

Saith, that he carried in the *Adventure Gally* from New-York, 154 Men; Seventy whereof came out of England with him. Some of his Sloop's Company put two Bailes of Goods on shore at Gardner's Island, being their own proper. The Narrator deliverd a Chest of Goods, *viz.* Muslins, Latches, Romals and flowered Silke, unto Mr. Gardner of Gardner's-Island aforesaid, to be kept there for the Narrator, put no Goods on shore any-where else. Several of his Company landed their Chests and other Goods at several places.

Further saith, He delivered a small Bayle of course Callicoes unto a Sloop-Man of Rhode-Island that he had emploied there. The Gold seized at Mr. Campbell's the Narrator intended for Presents to some that he expected to do him Kindness. Some of his Company put their Chests and Bailes on board a New York Sloop lying at Gardner's Island. Wm. Kidd

19

Bellomont's Secret

In private, Bellomont revealed a secret he had been keeping for seven months. He told the lieutenant governor and some of the members of the council that he received a letter from Secretary Vernon relaying the lords justices' disdain for Kidd's behavior while he was on his privateering voyage.[1] His treacherous acts of piracy in the Indian Ocean, particularly his taking the *Quedah Merchant*, were antithetical to his assignment to wage war on the pirates. Vernon ordered Bellomont to immediately arrest Kidd and his crew and to seize and secure the treasure.

Vernon's letter put Bellomont in a position as uncomfortable as his gout. Kidd had embarrassed Bellomont and his other high-ranking investors, but the treasure he'd secured was catnip—a tempting solution to Bellomont's pecuniary problems that would appease his wife. Despite his popularity among his fellow Bostonians, Bellomont couldn't convince the elected representatives to give him a permanent salary, and he did not appreciate the piddling amount they gave him for his annual "present."[2] In New York, the situation was no better. Being governor of the colonies was a prestigious but impractical undertaking. Uncertain of just what to do about Kidd, Bellomont waited to see how things played out before answering Vernon.

Kidd had been at large in Boston for six days, and he was beginning to grow paranoid. He told Sarah that Bellomont was acting distant and evasive. He had given the governor everything he asked for, but still there was no talk of a pardon.

On the morning of July 6 Kidd and his young enslaved worker went to Captain Way's Boston home to retrieve Sarah's money. Way described in a deposition that the money was in a "coarse canvas bag with two seals, and about the bigness of the crown of my hat and containing reals of eight for [Kidd's] wife to pay her charges."[3] Way had already delivered the other items in the pirate's wife survival kit to Sarah at the Campbells' house. After the pickup, Kidd returned to the Campbells' house and gave the money to Sarah who stored it in her traveling trunk with the other valuables she brought from New York. Later that day, Kidd went to Bellomont's residence to speak with him about his aloof behavior and initiate the discussion of a pardon.

What happened next is recorded in a letter from Bellomont to the Board of Trade: "Kidd was by the door of my lodging, and he rushed in, and came running to me, the constable after him…he seemed much disturbed…and fancied he looked as if he were upon the wing and resolved to run away…the gentlemen of the Council had the same thought… so I took their consent in seizing and committing him."[4]

It is hard to know if Kidd was as manic as Bellomont reported or if Bellomont was embellishing the story to justify his actions. Kidd reported that on July 6 he was forcibly removed from Bellomont's residence by the constables and put in the prison keeper's house next to the prison where others accused of piracy or aiding and corresponding with pirates were held.

20

Imprisoned

When Bellomont learned Kidd was in the prison keeper's house, he had him moved to the prison on the south side of Court Street to eliminate any chance of him escaping.[1] He did not want a repeat performance of what happened a few days before Kidd arrived in Boston when the pirates Joseph Bradish and Tee Witherly charmed the maid, Kate Price, into unlocking their cell at the prison keeper's house. Their clever escape was the talk of the town and even Judge Samuel Sewell noted it in his diary: "Bradish and Witherly brought to Town and sent to Prison, from whence they escaped June, 24."[2]

Bellomont wrote to the Board of Trade that "Kidd had a great deal of gold, which is apt to tempt men that have not principles of honour; I have therefore, to try the power of dull Iron against gold, put him in Irons that weight 16 pounds."[3] To ensure that Kidd remained chained in solitary confinement with sixteen pound weights, he boosted the sheriff's pay to forty shillings a week.[4]

When Kidd did not return from his meeting with Bellomont, Sarah became concerned. She was likely at Duncan Campbell's house with the children expecting him to walk through the door at any moment and ready to spend the evening together. It's not clear how she learned her husband had been thrown in jail, but Duncan Campbell may have been the messenger informed by Bellomont. The thought of Kidd chained like an animal in solitary confinement must have made her blood boil. When she calmed down, she may have said a prayer for his quick release.

Bellomont wrote to Secretary Vernon informing him of Kidd's arrest. He noted that in the many interviews he had had with Kidd, he was surprised by "the many lyes and Contradictions he told."[5] He explained that the reason he did not seize Kidd sooner, as he had been ordered, was because Kidd "had brought his wife and children hither in the sloop with him and I believed he would not easily forsake."[6]

Sarah and Kidd's relationship did not fit the stereotype of a pirate and his wife. In the literature of the time, pirates were portrayed as hypermasculine men whose interest in women was, for the most part, purely carnal. Sarah and Kidd had a relationship so strong that even by-the-book Bellomont recognized he had to give them some space. Sarah's presence delayed Kidd's capture. If she had not been with Kidd in Boston, he would have been seized immediately. Their mutual devotion unknowingly bought them more time together, something they would later learn, was more precious than all the treasure on the *Saint Antonio*.

With Kidd locked up, Bellomont ordered the council to seize the *Saint Antonio* and to place all of its contents in a safe place. He ordered his magistrates to search and seize treasure from Duncan Campbell's house and Sarah and Kidd's bed-room. The magistrates broke open Sarah's traveling trunk and absconded with her "silver tankard, a silver mugg, a silver porringer and spoons, forks, and 260 pieces of eight," and Elizabeth Morris's life savings of twenty-five English crowns.[7] Kidd's clothing and the contents of his chest containing "two silver basons, two silver candlesticks and one silver porringer" were also confiscated.[8] The raid made it abundantly clear to Sarah that her legal status had changed; she was now officially a pirate's wife and she and Kidd were viewed as a criminal couple.

21

The Pirate's Wife

Bellomont ordered Sarah arrested and taken to prison. The constables came to Campbell's house and barged into her bedroom. It is unlikely she went easily. Like Kidd who fought the constables and had to be dragged away with his heels leaving tracks behind in the dusty road while he shouted the curse words Bellomont forbade, Sarah probably tried to wrestle free from the men who grabbed her. Shoving and elbowing, maybe in sensitive places, Sarah struggled until several men overpowered her. They may have tied her wrists together behind her back to subdue her. Seeing her precious children, she may have leaned forward to touch each one's cheek with her face. The men may have arched her back to prevent the contact. Their brutal insensitivity may have brought Sarah into a high-pitched scream of anger—red-faced rage—as she begged them to let her go. But no doubt Sarah pleaded her innocence and demanded to know why she was being arrested and treated like a hardened criminal. Elizabeth and little Sarah saw their mother taken by armed guards and loaded into a horse-drawn wagon. Elizabeth Morris was there and cared for the girls while both their parents were in the stone prison. The violence of the break-in, the seizing of personal items, and the assault on their mother was traumatic for the little English girls who, just a few days ago, had the new experience of reuniting with a man they barely remembered as their father.

In her depressed state, Sarah could only hope she would not be in prison long and that soon she could comfort her daughters. She hoped, too, of course, Kidd would be released. Then they could get out of this miserable town and away from the horrible people.

Kidd was in solitary confinement and didn't know that Sarah was in the same putrid building locked in a cell with men and women whose crimes ranged from skipping out on church to murder.[1] Her security and honor were in the hands of two men—the prison keeper and the governor.

The inmates were given bread and water but additional food had to be purchased. Bellomont's men seized Sarah's money and with Kidd in prison unable to help her, she desperately needed funds to buy food. She secretly resorted to the backup plan Kidd had arranged with Captain Thomas Paine—the elderly retired pirate-turned–esteemed citizen–turned–Kidd's private banker—in the event that things went sour with the authorities. Sarah knew she could reach him through the pirate network.

On July 18, 1699, Sarah sent a letter from prison to Paine asking him to give seven bars of gold weighing twenty-four ounces to Andrew Knott, a pirate who lived in Boston and who was a friend and associate of James Gilliam, the murderous pirate passenger who was on board the *Saint Antonio*.

Sarah asked Paine to keep the rest of the gold in his custody until further notice "for it is all we have to support us in time of want."[2] Andrew Knott was instructed to deliver the gold bars to Sarah's maid who was minding the children at Duncan Campbell's house.

Sarah knew Paine would understand the seriousness of her request; Captain Kidd had made it clear during his visit to Paine's farm that leaving gold with Paine was an emergency backup plan to protect his wife and family. Paine could put two and two together: with both Sarah and Kidd in prison, this was an extreme situation—they had to tap into their reserves. Kidd's Boston lawyer may have written Sarah's letter to Captain Paine for her. It reads:[3]

> From Boston Prison, July ye 18 day 1699.
> Capt Payen,
> After my humble service to yr selfe and all our good Friends this cometh by a trusty Friend of mine how [sic] can declare to you of my great griefe and misery here in prison by how I would desire you to send me Twenty four ounces of Gold and as for all ye rest you have in your custody shall Desire you for to keep in your custody for it is all we have to support us in time of want; but I pray you to deliver to the bearer hereof the above-mentioned sum, hows name is Andrew Knott. And in so doing you will oblige him how is you're the bare hereof can informe you more at large.
> Sarah X S.K. X Keede.

Meanwhile, Lord Bellomont was combing Boston for pirates from Kidd's crew, including the notorious Red Sea pirate, James Gilliam. He and his men went to Andrew Knott's house demanding to know if Gilliam had been hiding out there.[4] Knott lied and said he had not seen Gilliam. Bellomont questioned Mrs. Knott, who, intimidated by the governor and his henchmen, admitted that Gilliam had spent several nights in their spare bedroom. As they spoke, Gilliam was not far from the Knotts' house. He was returning from a night of "friendly" activity with two young Boston women[5] (while his wife was in London). Bellomont and his men searched the Knotts' house for any stolen loot Gilliam may have left and to their surprise, they found Sarah's letter to Captain Paine buried in a wooden trunk under some remnants of East India goods.[6]

Bellomont had received a tip from an Admiralty Court judge in Rhode Island that Captain Paine had had a visit from Kidd and might be involved in receiving and concealing stolen goods.[7] After confiscating Sarah's letter, Bellomont no doubt had Paine in his crosshairs.

Andrew Knott quickly rode his horse past farms and villages to Paine's farm on Conanicut Island, a mile west of Newport, Rhode Island, to get the news to Paine that Bellomont was onto him. He handed Paine Sarah's desperate letter and told him that Bellomont had found it hidden in a trunk. It was just a matter of time before he would be at his door. Paine disappeared into a back room in his house and retrieved the seven bars of gold Sarah requested. They weighed twenty-four ounces.

Knott rode swiftly to Campbell's house and delivered the gold. He testified that he:

Went to Captain Payne's house on Conicut Island and received from Captain Payne 7 bars of gold weighting 1 — lb., being weighed by a pair of Steelyards. Payne fetched the gold from out of an inner room (or bed-room) and took Knott's receipt. Knot saw no more gold than what Payne brought out, and upon the Road in his way homeward, the weight of the gold broke his pocket, and he lost one of the bars. The other six he brought to Boston and Captain Kidd's servant maiden, Rebecca, came to Captain Kidd's house and fetched the gold to Kidd, who later on gave Knot 20 pieces of eight for his jornie and trouble. The jornie took 5 days.[8]

Sarah's maid used the scale from her pirate's wife survival kit to weigh it. There were six bars that weighed 21½ or 22 ounces. She would have wanted to know what happened to the seventh bar. Knott testified that one of the bars broke through his pocket and fell to the ground on his way home from the five-day journey. Sarah doubted his story but was helpless to do anything about it. She was in prison trying to survive. More than likely, Captain Knott kept the gold bar for himself as remuneration for his favor to Sarah.

How long Sarah languished in jail is unclear; it was more than a few days, and may have been about a week. Bellomont considered Sarah the wife of a scoundrel and he had every reason to believe she was like the company she kept. Finally, however, Bellomont had to admit that he had no evidence to justify her arrest and she was released from prison. When her cell was unlocked and the jailer informed her she was free, she must have felt enormous relief, as well as anger and disgust for having been held captive. She had been locked up in tight quarters with people who all smelled of sweat, urine, and whatever was in the hole in the ground that passed as their toilet. With dirty disheveled hair, she returned home in the same dress she wore when she was arrested. Her daughters had to be taken aback at the sight of her.

Duncan Campbell urged Sarah to send a petition to Bellomont and the council to return her belongings that were seized on July 6. It was risky for Campbell to involve himself in the affairs of a couple in trouble with the law, but rather than shy away from the Kidds, he gave Sarah detailed advice on how to go about approaching the governor and his council. She would soon learn how it was that Duncan Campbell was so familiar with Bellomont. But for now, as a woman and an outsider in Boston, Sarah needed the help of an inside man.

Sarah's original petition remains in the Massachusetts State Archives in Boston and you can see where she scratched her initials into the paper with deep, almost violent etches. Maybe the quill pen was new and especially sharp, preventing the black ink from flowing easily across the page, but more than likely Sarah was so incensed and outraged by the way she was treated as a pirate's wife that she strained to control herself. She may not have been able to write her name, but she knew what she wanted to say and she dictated her message clearly. Her petition reads:[9]

July 18, 1699
To his Excellency the Earl of Bellomont, Captn. Gen. and Govr. In Chief of his Maj'tys provinces of the Massachu-

setts Bay, New Yorke, etca. In America, and of the Territorys thereon depending, and Vice Admiral of the same,

The petition of Sarah Kidd, the wife of Captain Wm. Kidd:

Humbly Sheweth:

That on the sixth day of July Inst. some of the Magistrates and officers of this place came into your Pet'rs lodgings at the house of Duncan Campbell and did there Seize and take out of a Trunck a Silver Tankard, a Silver Mugg, Silver Porringer, spoons, forcks and other pieces of Plate, and two hundred and sixty pieces of Eight, your Pet'rs sole and proper Plate and mony, brought with her from New Yorke, whereof she has had the possession for several years last past, as she can truly make oath; out of which sd Trunck was also took Twenty five English Crowns which belonged to your Pet'rs Maid.

The premises and most deplorable Condition of yr. Pet'r considered, She humbly intreats your hon'rs Justice, That Returne be made of the said Plate and mony.

Sarah X (S.K.) X Kidd

Sarah's petition was included in the council records with a notation confirming her request. The council "Advised that Mrs. Kidd makeing oath that she brought the Plate and money above mentioned from New York with her, It was restored unto her. And also that Capn. Kidd and Companys wearing Apparel under Seizure be returned to them."[10]

This was a major victory for Sarah—she regained her silver. The pirate's wife took on the colonial authorities and won. This is significant because under the English law of coverture married women did not have legal rights of their own. Imprisoned, Kidd could not protect Sarah and provide the legal umbrella as the head of household. She fought for what was rightfully hers, and she wasn't going to let Bellomont, who represented the patriarchal authority in society, take away her individual rights. For now, at least, Sarah had regained her footing after being assaulted physically, emotionally, and legally.

The constables returned the two trunks. She put hers with the silver, and Kidd's with his clothing, back where they belonged in their borrowed bedroom. Now that their belongings were restored, she could focus on how to get her husband out of prison. She may have sat on the bed and closed her eyes to think through who was friend and who was foe. Getting Kidd out of jail was a dangerous undertaking and only a devoted and loyal friend would risk getting involved. And she needed money for bribes—the wink and a nod everyone understood.

Sarah asked Elizabeth Morris to go see Thomas Clark and retrieve the sack of gold Kidd secretly gave him in June when he was hovering around Gardiner's Island.[11] They needed the money to bribe the jailer. It turned out that Clark gave the £10,000 of Kidd's money and East India goods to Major Jonathan Selleck who had a warehouse in Stamford, Connecticut, near the water, a convenient spot to receive items from vessels.[12] Clark refused to retrieve any of the money that was hidden in the warehouse. He had already been arrested by Bellomont once[13] and he was afraid the governor would do it again and this time it would not be a temporary stay. To protect himself, he denied any involvement with the treasure and said "the goods delivered to him were from Madame Kidd."[14]

His claim was far from the truth. Clark was on board the *Saint Antonio* with Sarah and it was *he* who transferred chests of treasure to the waiting New York sloop. He then boarded the same sloop and left a full day before Sarah and Kidd departed Gardiner's Island. Gardiner reported that he saw Clark leave in the sloop that contained "the chests of treasure and other goods."[15] The man who had showed some courtly manners escorting Sarah to Block Island had ultimately betrayed her. Fearing Kidd would retaliate if he was ever released from prison,[16] Clark eventually agreed to return all of Kidd's goods to Bellomont on the condition that Bellomont assure him that Kidd would be put in irons on a prison ship to England.

Sarah realized she could not make the escape plan alone. She needed Kidd's help and she would tell him about Clark's betrayal. He would know where he stashed more money. With the help of her lawyer, Sarah sent another petition on July 25, 1699, to Bellomont and the council requesting permission to visit her husband in jail because "he being under strait durance and in want of necessary assistance, as well as from your Petitioners Affection to her husband."[17] Sarah's efforts showed her resilience and determination to bring Kidd home. Her daughters may have been too young to understand these important values in their mother, but they certainly would remember the events in Boston and later appreciate that she was hell-bent on keeping their family together. They witnessed their mother's love for their family and for their father, who, despite his faults that resulted in this whole disastrous affair, she was standing by. Sarah's petition to Bellomont reads:[18]

To his Excell'cy the Earle of Bellomont, Capt. Gen'll and Governor of his Maj'tys Collonies of the Massachusetts Bay in N. Engl'd etca. and to the honorable the Councill.

The Peticion of Sarah Kidd humbly Sheweth

That Your Petitioners husband Capt. Wm. Kidd, being committed unto the Comon Goale in Boston for Pyracie, and under Streight durance, as Alsoe in want of necessary Assistance, as well as from your Petitioners Affection to her husband humbly pray's that your Excell'cy and Councill will be pleased to permit the sd Sarah Kidd to have Communication with her husband, for his reliefe; in such due Season and maner, as by your Excelle'y and Councill may be tho't fit and prescribed, to which Your Petitioner shall thankfully conforme herSelfe and ever pray etca.

SARAH SK KIDD Boston 25 July 1699

The wording was appropriate; Bellomont knew how close Sarah and Kidd were. It was only natural she would want to comfort Kidd while he was under duress, chained to the wall in solitary confinement. Bellomont was married; he may have known some tenderness with his wife, Countess Kate Bellomont. Sarah was hopeful he would step out of his role as governor and see her request as a compassionate and understanding human being. What she didn't tell Bellomont, of course, was that in addition to comforting her husband, she wanted to help him plan an escape. Sarah was using Bellomont, luring him with her charm, just like he had lured them to Boston under false pretenses. She was playing cat and mouse with him, a shrewd move under the cover of sweet marital love. Her street-savvy smarts were at full power. Now that she knew firsthand the inside of the prison, she knew where the doors and windows were, who came and went, and the overall daily routine of the jail keeper. This was valuable intelligence she learned the hard way, but now it came in handy.

Kidd befriended the jailer, Caleb Ray, with his affable personality. He hoped his influence and Sarah's charm and emergency money from Captain Paine would persuade Ray to help him escape.

Suspecting they would collude on an escape plan, Bellomont denied Sarah's petition to visit Kidd. He also caught wind of Kidd's friendship with the jailer and had Caleb Ray reassigned. He even offered Kidd's Boston lawyer, Thomas Newton, a plumb job outside of Boston so that Sarah and Kidd would not have access to first-rate legal counsel. To further isolate Kidd from any outside influences, he was moved deeper into the prison, making it more difficult for Sarah to communicate with him through the window.

Bellomont lost no time hunting down those who had come in contact with Sarah and Kidd. He had read Sarah's letter to Captain Paine; he went to Rhode Island to interview him.[19] Sarah had instructed Paine to keep safe the extra gold left over from the seven bars he gave to Andrew Knott.

This led Bellomont to believe there was still a good deal of treasure in Paine's custody.[20] Bellomont tried to depose Paine three or four times but he refused.[21] It was only under threat of jail that Paine swore that he rebuffed Kidd's request to conceal his gold. That was a lie; he did not refuse Kidd, but he was in a tough spot and the choice was either to lie or get arrested for concealing stolen goods. At the time, a lie seemed the lesser of two evils. He was committed to helping Sarah and keeping her confidences in her time of need.

Even though Bellomont doubted Paine's story and found his behavior "extremely disordered and believed that he did not swear nice truth,"[22] he left well enough alone and did not persist in questioning or threatening Paine. Bellomont did not have jurisdiction in Rhode Island and Paine was well-connected—his father-in-law was the former governor. Bellomont believed Paine still had "a great deal more of Kidd's goods still in his hands [but] he is out of my power and being in that government I cannot compel him to deliver up the [rest]."[23] Bellomont reported that the government of Rhode Island was the "most irregular and illegal in their administration that ever any English Government was."[24]

For now, Sarah's secret was safe and so was her money. What a relief for her to know there was one secure place where she could access her funds in the future. Paine hid his friend's gold where no one of authority could find it. He lived on a large wooded farm on the north end of Conanicut Island, in Jamestown, Rhode Island. A photograph of the historic house shows that it faced east overlooking Narragansett Bay, and the rocky shoreline was just a few hundred feet from the front door of the hewn oak–framed two-story house with a gabled roof and center chimney.[25] When Kidd initially visited him, he sailed close to the house in the *Saint Antonio* and sent a small boat to shore, according to local records. Paine's house, where he lived with his wife, Mercy Carr Paine, would have been easy for Kidd to find because the second floor had an overhanging roof, an unusual feature for a house built on Conanicut Island in the 1690s. The house was built with a large room on each floor. The center chimney warmed the entire house and it is possible that Paine hid the gold bars in a crawl space beneath the wide plank floors of the house, a root cellar, or an "inner room" as Knott called it, where Mercy kept her preserved fruits and vegetables. Wherever it was, it was Paine's chosen secret place where gold did not glisten. The grizzled Paine was well practiced at hiding stolen loot, and his reputation as the trusted pirate banker continued after he retired from being "on the account" because he was so skilled at navigating between the lines of the law.

In New York, the authorities also questioned Dorothy Lee. There is no record of her reaction when Bellomont's uniformed men knocked on the Pearl Street door and asked to speak with her. She must have been horrified to learn what had happened to Sarah and Kidd—worried sick that she would never see Sarah and the children again. The questioning put a fine point on Ms. Lee's long tenure with Sarah: she had known her since she was a teenager and married to a merchant, and now, a decade later, she was minding the house of a pirate's wife. Dorothy Lee denied she knew anything about goods from Kidd's vessel.[26] She may have been telling the truth, or maybe not. She was devoted to Sarah and it's conceivable that she would have lied to protect her, just as Thomas Paine had.

There is no record that Sarah or Kidd sent any treasure home, but that does not mean that they didn't. It would make good sense if, during the time when Kidd was distributing treasure to various people in Connecticut and Rhode Island, he sent one of his trusted emissaries to New York to surreptitiously ensure that Sarah had money when she returned from Boston. Kidd may have sent the portion of the treasure that he considered his share of the fortune. He would not have sent large portions of the treasure to New York City because his leverage with Bellomont depended on the governor imagining his own financial boon with a share of Kidd's treasure.

Dorothy Lee may have hidden treasure in the eaves of the attic—the place where Emott first told Sarah that her husband was in home waters and accused of turning pirate. Kidd knew exactly how much space was available—he'd used the attic to store his cargo when he was a merchant sea captain. There were places that were not obvious to the untrained eye that would conceal some of Kidd's newfound cargo—a detail a longtime housekeeper would know.

Based on the generous gifts he gave Countess Kate Bellomont and Susannah Campbell it is very likely that Kidd had an extraspecial gift for Sarah. Such a gift may have been secretly transferred to Dorothy Lee with the other treasure for safekeeping. Then, if Kidd returned to New York with Sarah, he could give her the present himself. History records that Kidd was a prudent man who planned for contingencies; he also was sentimental and protective of his wife.

★ ★ ★

Bellomont learned that a great deal of Kidd's treasure was on Gardiner's Island and that one of Kidd's men—possibly sent by Sarah—offered £30 for a sloop to carry him to Gardiner's Island to retrieve the buried gold.[27] In a race against the clock to see who would get to the treasure first, Bellomont quickly dispatched a messenger with an order in the king's name telling Gardiner that Kidd was in prison and he must come to Boston immediately with the treasure.[28] Bellomont's messenger traveled at breakneck speed and reached Gardiner's Island before Kidd's man could dig up the buried treasure.[29]

Kidd had confided in Gardiner the location of the buried treasure—it was in a ravine in the heavily wooded forest between Bostwick's Point and the manor house. Gardiner knew every inch of his property and found it easily. With the help of his workers, Gardiner had Kidd's chest of gold unearthed. He collected all the other goods he was holding for Kidd and took the bounty of 1111 ounces of gold, 2353 ounces of silver, spices, Goa stones, and silk quilts with tassels to Boston. Judge Sewell and four members of the council were assigned to keep watch over the storehouse where Kidd's treasure was stored and secured with a very strong lock.[30]

Sarah learned Duncan Campbell and Bellomont were on friendly terms, so friendly, the Campbells entertained Bellomont at their fine home just a few weeks before the Kidds arrived.[31] The connection may not have registered with Sarah at first. She met Campbell through Kidd during the tense exchange of letters on the *Saint Antonio*. Campbell seemed genuinely interested in helping Kidd, and Sarah knew that her husband trusted him. What she didn't know was that Campbell not only delivered letters back and forth between Kidd and Bellomont, but as the postmaster for the largest and most important seaport in British America, he used his office for a broader purpose. Since 1693, when the Glasgow, Scotland, native was appointed to the position, he not only received and dispatched the mail, but he made it his business to collect information from faraway places. He was in contact with the masters of incoming ships who came to Boston with news they'd picked up in the form of hearsay reports and the London prints—newspapers and pamphlets.[32] Campbell was charming, fashionable, and popular among the Boston elite.[33] He was also a self-serving informant who used his official post to obtain juicy gossip and curry favor with the governor. When Sarah learned that it was Campbell who told Bellomont about the treasure on Gardiner's Island, she packed her bags and she, her daughters, and maid took a room at a humble waterfront inn near the prison.[34] Sarah never spoke to Campbell again.[35]

Kidd proposed to Bellomont—through the jail keeper— that he be sent as a prisoner to Hispaniola to bring back the *Quedah Merchant*, which he estimated carried about £50,000–60,000 worth of treasure.[36] As the ship was a lawful prize, Bellomont and his fellow investors would receive four-fifths of the take. Without Kidd, the treasure would be lost. He hoped the proposition would entice Bellomont, but the governor told Kidd that he would consider no such proposition from a "King's Prisoner."[37] He later told his colleagues in London on the Board of Trade, "there never was a great Lyar or Thief in the World than this Kidd."[38] Meanwhile, however, Bellomont egged on the jail keeper to try to wheedle out of Kidd the location of the ship and treasure in Hispaniola.[39]

Months passed and Sarah waited for her husband to be released. Boston was experiencing an especially cold fall and Kidd spent all but thirty minutes a day in solitary confinement. Kidd was always on Sarah's mind and knowing the harsh conditions in the prison, she imagined Kidd would be suffering in his cold damp cell, curled up in a corner on the dirt floor fighting to stay warm. It was an impossible battle especially with the cold sixteen-pound manacles rubbing the open sores on his ankles and wrists.

On October 12, 1699, Sarah sent a petition to the governor and council requesting that Kidd be given warm clothes. She was hoping, for more than one reason, she could see her husband and bring him the warm clothes herself. Sarah may have had something to tell him. A stirring in her belly. A familiar and happy event, under normal circumstances.

Genealogical research shows Sarah gave birth to a baby girl named Mary Kidd sometime in 1700.[40] Given their time together from their reunion on Block Island in late June 1699 to his capture on July 6, it is entirely possible that she conceived a child. She would be near the end of her first trimester now and aware of her new condition. Sarah's concern for Kidd's welfare is all the more poignant with her pregnancy: she wanted and needed him to survive the cold so he could live to see their new child, their third daughter. Birth records in Boston and New York have not survived to verify the date and location of the birth. And because there are so few records about baby Mary, and she is not mentioned in Sarah's will written late in her life naming her five children, it is very likely the baby did not survive infancy, or if she did, she did not reach adulthood.

The Council of Trade and Plantations in London ordered that clothing for Kidd and the prisoners be provided and paid for out of Kidd's treasure.[41] Unfortunately, Sarah was not allowed to deliver the clothes to Kidd (and maybe sneak in a blanket). She could only hope there would be another opportunity to see him and share her—their—news. Meanwhile, Sarah was likely relieved the request was approved, at least.

If it wasn't for Sarah, the stonehearted governor would not have thought of Kidd's suffering. Bellomont did ultimately send through the request to the Council of Trade and Plantations, but he did not give Sarah the credit she was due: he didn't tell Kidd it was Sarah's idea to move his arrival port to New York and he probably didn't tell Kidd it was Sarah's petition that brought about his getting warm clothes.

Christmas 1699 was a nonevent for Sarah's family. Kidd had been in prison five months and Sarah and the girls were in a holding pattern waiting for his release. Sarah was now widely perceived as a pirate's wife, an associate to an outlaw, and a disgraced socialite. Her good standing now diminished, she was also now a single parent. Perhaps she thought of her life up to now—she had gone from being the wife of two merchants to the wife of a notorious outlaw. Just twenty-nine years old, she had already lived a very full life.

As the winter wore on, Bellomont grew more and more anxious about holding Kidd in Boston's prison. Under Massachusetts law, piracy was not a hanging offense.[42] In England, it was. Bellomont wanted to change the Massachusetts law to conform to the laws of England so he could prosecute the pirates and be done with them.[43] "These pirates I have in jail make me very uneasy for fear they should escape. I would give £100 if they were all in Newgate," Bellomont wrote the authorities in England referring to the grisly prison in London.[44]

On Tuesday, February 6, 1700, a frigid and windy day, Bellomont assembled his council to take a vote to change the Massachusetts law. He argued that "piracy grows daily"[45] and he feared that the people were so favorable to pirates that there could be no justice against them.[46]

Bellomont knew that when pirates escaped, or were never caught in the first place, it was hard to capture them because they returned home and found protection. Pirates' wives, families, and communities wrapped their arms around them, so to speak, providing shelter and emotional support. Many citizens shook their heads "no" when asked by Bellomont's constables if they had seen pirates. Harboring pirates on-the-run, as the Knotts did for James Gilliam, was part of the pirate culture. And, as previously discussed, pirates provided useful services to the community at large. It was only Bellomont and his like that declared war on the pirates. Many thought pirates were acceptable neighbors.

Bellomont did not win the unanimous vote he sought. Judge Sewell and two others on the council voted against changing the law.[47] Sewell wrote in his diary, "I knew of no power I had to send men out of the province [to be tried for piracy]."[48] If Sarah knew of Sewell's position she would have been relieved. At least there was someone aside from her who believed the law should not be changed just to suit the will of the frustrated and impatient governor. While Bellomont lost the vote to change the law, he received orders from the king to transport Kidd and the other pirates to England for trial. If he were found guilty, he could be hanged.

22

The King's Ship

The *Rochester* sailed from London to pick up Kidd and the other pirates in Boston's prison,[1] but the ship was battered by a storm 500 leagues out (about 1,726 miles) and was forced to turn back. The Admiralty immediately ordered a replacement and the HMS *Advice*, a fourth-rate warship with forty guns and a crew of 197 men set sail.

Discouraged that Thomas Clark had turned on him and would not release his gold, Kidd continued to work on an escape. One plan was for "the lovely and accomplished" Sarah to use her charm to sweet-talk the jailor into unlocking the hard chains rubbing the open sores on his ankles and wrists. The other plan was for Kidd to try to persuade the jailer himself. It is uncertain which plan worked, but the jailer took off the irons on Wednesday, February 8, 1700, out of compassion for Kidd's aching body. The next step was for Sarah to figure out how to loosen the bars so Kidd could slip by, or get the guards drunk so she could open the cell door herself in the dark of night. Time was of the essence. The HMS *Advice* had arrived in Boston harbor.

The Kidds planned an escape for five days hence—February 13—but they still had to figure out how to do it. Could Sarah smuggle Kidd a gun, or a knife, or a file? Or could Kidd persuade the jailor, now a compassionate soul, to allow Sarah and Kidd a private visit together—it had been months since they had seen each other—and together they could plan the getaway?

The days were so unseasonably frigid that the harbor was icing over. Judge Sewell recorded in his diary that the days were the coldest in Boston's recent history. Bellomont was anxious to get the prisoners out of his colony and onto the king's ship. Bradish and Witherly, who had escaped, were recaptured and in prison, as was James Gilliam.[2] Bellomont knew he was dealing with very clever and determined men intent on escaping. Kidd wanted nothing else than to get out of prison and be with Sarah.

The weather made it impossible to get the pirates on board quickly. A dramatic shift in temperature melted the ice, briefly unleashing a huge ice sheet more than several hundred feet long. It rammed into the *Advice*, eventually beaching it. Boston mariners had to help right the ship and ferry it out to deep water in the harbor.

Kidd had been out of shackles five days, since February 8, but Sarah hadn't figured out how, even with the help of the pirate network, to get him out of his cell.[3] Bellomont was weary from his poor health and distrustful of Kidd. He sent a man to check on him. When he learned that Kidd was unshackled and moving about his cell, Bellomont immediately demanded Kidd be reshackled and set the date of the HMS *Advice*'s departure for February 16, 1700.

Bellomont did his planning in secret. Captain Robert Winn of the Royal Navy was in charge and given special orders pertaining to Kidd; he was to be in isolation so that he could not receive or give information. If anything leaked out from Kidd it would jeopardize the reputations of those high-ranking authorities that had sponsored his privateering voyage. And Bellomont, too, would be exposed for his part in the Kidd affair and have to explain his complicated relationship with the man he held in chains for so long. By keeping Kidd quiet, the authorities attempted to quash any potential political scandal. Captain Winn kept a journal and recorded the details of his historic assignment. His journal, and the journal of his second lieutenant, Thomas Langrish, who safeguarded the treasure aboard the HMS *Advice*, have survived and give insight into the events that transpired on those frigid days in February 1700.

Bellomont was not present when his men unlocked Kidd's cell, unshackled him, and forced him out of the prison. He was in poor health and likely would've avoided the germ-infested prison, especially during a cold snap. But by staying away he didn't have to make eye contact with the man he betrayed.

Kidd put up a fight as he was taken out, as he did when he was first captured in Bellomont's residence. He still professed he was not a pirate.

By the time Sarah awoke at the inn, her husband was gone. The jail keeper probably left his cell door open, so that the stench from his more than seven months of captivity could dissipate. Kidd and thirty-one other pirates were tied up and rowed out five miles to where the HMS *Advice* was anchored between Bullock's Island and Sheep's Island in Boston Harbor.[4] Nine of them—Edward Davis, James Gilliam, Gabriel Loff, Samuel Arris, Hugh Parrot, Robert Lamley, William Jenkins, Joseph Palmer, and Richard Barleycorn[5]—were Kidd's associates and accomplices from the *Saint Antonio*, and Sarah knew each of them. Per Bellomont's orders, Kidd was put in isolation and chained in a cabin in steerage. With him were his two young enslaved Malagasy children, a boy and a girl.[6] It is not known why Kidd was allowed to have his young enslaved workers with him, but the fact that even an accused criminal was still allowed to own children underscores the horror of slavery. The children were on board with other accused criminals and likely living in the same conditions or worse.

But the HMS *Advice* did not sail immediately. There were repairs to be made to the rigging and sails, more prisoners to board, food to store, and lastly, Kidd's treasure to load. The official tally, recorded in the State Papers at the Public Record Office in London, estimated Kidd's treasure to be worth £14,000.[7] Bellomont had retrieved every bit he could find, even Countess Kate Bellomont's and Susannah Campbell's gifts from Kidd were confiscated.[8]

On Wednesday, February 28, 1700, Kidd's treasure was removed from the storehouse and loaded on the *Saint Antonio*, which was tied up on the "outward wharf," Sewell reported in his diary, grateful that the storehouse had not been broken into or "no fire happened." It is uncertain if Sarah went near the storehouse and watched the undoing of all of her plans with Kidd. She would have seen some of the things she inventoried going back into the hold of the *Saint*

Antonio. Oddly, things had come full circle. Kidd's ship was sailed out to the HMS *Advice* where the treasure was transferred under careful guard to the cargo area.

Along with his treasure, Captain Kidd was transferred to the HMS *Advice*, where he was held prisoner in Boston Harbor for three weeks. Captain Winn made daily trips from the ship to the governor's residence, meeting Bellomont at 7:00 a.m. and staying until evening to keep apprised of the trip plans.[9] In the freezing cold, amid floating chunks of ice, his men rowed him back and forth. The commute each way took several hours.

One afternoon, when Captain Winn was leaving Bellomont's residence, Sarah caught his attention and introduced herself.[10] It is very likely he already knew who she was: news of Sarah and Kidd's time in Boston was widely publicized in the colonies and abroad and Sarah's effort to save her husband and secure a pardon reached a London Tory newspaper with the two names, the *Flying Post* or the *Post Master*. "The Relations of Kid the Pirate are making great Intercession for his Pardon," they wrote.[11] Standing in the numbing cold wrapped in a blanket (she did not bring a winter coat with her when she left New York in June for Block Island), Sarah told Captain Winn she needed a favor. She wanted—needed—to get a message to her husband. She wished to say goodbye and send him her love, and to tell him what their love produced. She would be about seven months pregnant and showing but the thick wool covering may have disguised her bump. Captain Winn said that he could not deliver a message to Kidd because he was under such heavy guard.

He was a "close prisoner" he said, which meant he could not have visitors or receive letters.[12]

Sarah knew that gifts were often used to influence and persuade. She was well aware of Kidd's intent in sending Countess Kate Bellomont tokens of his esteem. From a small pouch, she took out a heavy gold ring and pressed it into Captain Winn's hand.[13] "I can deliver no message," Captain Winn said, and tried to give her back the ring.

Anyone watching them from a distance would have seen the intensity of their exchange. Sarah, the pirate's wife, speaking with a uniformed officer of His Majesty's Royal Navy. The air was so cold their breath formed clouds. Sarah pressed the ring into the palm of his hand. He tried to return the ring with his gloved hand. Winn saw a woman with so much pain in her eyes: her attractive features were worn and haggard from the challenges of her Boston experience. By her presence, though, he sensed her determined spirit. "Be kind to my husband," she said.[14] Sarah hoped she might convince Captain Winn to disregard his orders, just this once.

He was still holding the ring Sarah refused to take back. The longboat was waiting for him at the wharf. Captain Winn had to get back to the HMS *Advice* and make the final arrangements for its departure on March 10 to London. As Sarah walked away, she told Captain Winn he should keep the ring, "as a 'token' until we meet again…when you bring my husband back to me."[15]

23

Newgate

On March 10, 1700, the HMS *Advice* set sail for London. Kidd's departure from Boston was the talk of the town. Colonists could see the ship at full sail in the distance knowing it held the rogues Bellomont and the authorities in London hated. Sarah and the girls were likely among the onlookers. Per Kidd's request, they were to return to Manhattan and wait to hear any news from him.

Kidd arrived in London Sunday afternoon April 14, 1700, and was directed by the High Court of Admiralty to go aboard the yacht *Katherine* where he was to be escorted to Newgate prison to remain "until he shall be delivered by due course of law."[1]

Kidd was taken to the five-story stone building adjacent to the Old Bailey court building on the corner of Newgate and Old Bailey Street inside the City of London. Shackled at the ankles and wrists, he was again put in solitary confinement in a dark, damp foul-smelling cell that measured fifteen feet by twenty feet with a wooden platform for a bed. With him were his two young enslaved companions and records show the keeper of Newgate provided fresh food and clothing for them. The marshal who was watching over Kidd relayed to the Admiralty that Captain Kidd gave him a piece of gold and asked him to send it to his wife in New York.[2] Kidd believed he was going to die since his papers were gone and he wanted to make one last effort to take care of Sarah. The French Passes Emott gave to Lord Bellomont "disappeared" and were not available as evidence of Kidd's innocence. Kidd asked that he not suffer the shameful death of hanging but instead be shot or given a knife, which the marshal refused to do.[3] The marshal did not send Sarah Kidd's last gold piece. If it made it out of the marshal's pocket, it may have been added to the collection of Kidd's treasure.

The Admiralty postponed Kidd's case until the next session, leaving Kidd to languish in Newgate prison for over a year before he was tried. During that time, even though he had not been convicted they treated him like he was, not allowing him to have clean clothes, exercise, visitors, or access to pen and paper. After eight months confined in Boston and now in Newgate, Kidd was sick with body aches and fits that wracked his mind. By May, he was so ill the authorities thought he might die. Rather than lose the opportunity to bring him to trial, they granted him pen and paper, better food, and a visitor.

In May 1700, Mrs. Hawkins, a distant relative of Sarah's and Kidd's landlady in 1695 when he was in London to obtain a privateering commission, was allowed to visit in the presence of a jail keeper. Mrs. Hawkins had heard Kidd was in Newgate and in a desperate condition. She requested and received special permission to bring him a trunk of fresh clothes and she was allowed to care for him while he was ill.

Caring for Kidd in the disease-ridden prison had to have been a grim experience for Mrs. Hawkins. She saw a man who had once been so physically strong now weak and vulnerable. Kidd was deranged from the emotional and physical stress of his extended time in prisons. He must have been moved by her warmth, support, and compassion. To enter Newgate, she had to go through its ominous iron gate. She would have been stopped by the stench of the prisoners and the sight of eyes, desperate eyes, peering at her through the slits in their cells as she walked through the courtyard. She didn't have to go to see Kidd: she could have ignored the reports in the press of his bad health. But she remembered him fondly when he was vibrant and eager to sail under the king's jack and pendant as a privateer for His Majesty's government. Her affection for Kidd reflected her love for Sarah. Although distantly related, there was a connection between the two. Kidd may have seen the similarity in the nurturing and loving women; Mrs. Hawkins cared that he had clean clothes in Newgate just as Sarah cared that he had warm clothes in Boston prison. No doubt, Kidd and Mrs. Hawkins talked about Sarah and the children. He could tell her of their time together until it was abruptly cut short in Boston. Kidd's mind most likely wandered home, to Sarah and the children, to the four-poster bed with its soft quilt and goose down pillows and Sarah beside him. He had to have felt worried about Sarah all alone in New York. In his weakened state, he may have become emotional in front of Mrs. Hawkins; tears of anguish and fear wetting his cupped hands. Kidd's family in Dundee, Scotland, was far away from London and he had lost touch with them. Mrs. Hawkins *was* his family—a mother, sister, aunt, and cousin all in one. There is every reason to believe Mrs. Hawkins tried to reach Sarah to let her know about her visit with Kidd. Like Sarah, she may not have been able to write, but her husband, Matthew, ran a butcher shop and likely sent a letter. Sarah would have been happy to hear from her. She recently gave birth to baby Mary and she may have been feeling very alone.

24

Kidd's Good Deed

As Kidd faced an uncertain future his thoughts turned to two of his deceased crewmen. While he anguished in Newgate, he tried to help the wives of Henry Mead and William Beck, who had died in Madagascar five years earlier, at the start of his privateering voyage. In keeping with the articles, the personal effects of the men were sold at the mast to the highest bidder. Captain Kidd held the money from the auction for the wives, but Bellomont seized it when he was arrested. Captain Kidd sent Matthew Hawkins to find the widows in London.

The women petitioned the Lords of the Admiralty for permission to visit Captain Kidd at Newgate and they were told that "there was time enough for them to lay claim to what was due to them" and referred to the Keeper of Newgate to gain admittance to speak with Kidd.[1] The keeper tried to deny the widows' access but was compelled to grant them admittance after their appeal to the king. Elizabeth Mead and Gertrude Beck, accompanied by their lawyer, were finally given permission to visit Kidd.

Kidd explained the situation to the women and told them he would try to help them get their money from the Admiralty. This was important news to Elizabeth Mead who was on the verge of going to debtors' prison for the unpaid bill of £10 her husband accumulated in New York before he left for sea.[2] Captain Kidd gave them the details of the case: where and how the men had died, and the list of the personal effects that were sold. For Henry Mead, the well-dressed, well-read first mate on Kidd's ship, Kidd had received 900 pieces of eight for his personal effects. The inventory of his good taste reads like that of an English gentleman: "brandy, tobacco, sea charts, mathematical books and instruments, twenty other books, six new suits of clothes, very good linen and bedding, five light-colored wigs, three pair of silver shoe buckles, two sets of silver buttons for sleeves, with stones in them, three hats and a good quantity of sugar."[3] William Beck had similar cargo but not in the same quantity as Mead; his effects went for 450 pieces of eight.

The widows petitioned the High Court of Admiralty for their husbands' money in April 1701, but were refused. They petitioned directly to the king and were told that their request was read to King William but the king said he did not have the power to grant them their money and that they had to apply through the proper courts. Elizabeth Mead found a lawyer to press her claim in the High Court of Admiralty. She lost the case and it is highly likely that she went to debtors' prison.

25

Trial

Not long after Kidd was sent to London, Bellomont returned to New York to tend to the colony's business. His gout worsened and he died on Saturday, March 5, 1701. It is not known whether Kidd was informed of his nemesis's death—he was busy trying to save his own life. But Sarah certainly would have known because the public funeral was a lavish affair. Attendees received a ring with Bellomont's initials as the funeral gift,[1] and the procession ended at the fort near Sarah's Pearl Street home. Worse for Sarah, Bellomont was interred under the chapel,[2] a constant reminder of the ordeal she'd endured at his hand.

Duncan Campbell traveled from Boston to Manhattan with a letter of condolence from the Massachusetts Governor's Council for Bellomont's widow.[3] Kind words about her husband were little solace to Countess Bellomont who reported to Secretary Vernon that her husband's service to the Crown left her family financially destitute and "in a distressed condition."[4] We can imagine that Sarah felt little sympathy for the titled widow, who had access to the Crown for assistance.

Sarah may have thought that if Bellomont had stuck with his get-rich-quick plan, his wife wouldn't be complaining.

Kidd appeared before the House of Commons on March 27 and March 31 and pleaded for mercy. His claim that he "did not seek the [privateering] Commission...but was partly Cajoled, and partly menac'd into it by the Lord Bellomont and one Robert Livingston..."[5] fell on disinterested ears. It was during one of his appearances before the House of Commons that Sir James Thornhill, a portrait painter known for rendering historic figures, made a drawing of Kidd. It is the only true representation of Kidd that exists. He was dressed as a gentleman wearing a light brown shoulder-length wig parted down the middle, a fancy white dress shirt with a cravat, and a black coat. His straight brown eyebrows, jutting chin, pursed lips, and pointed nose cut a distinct profile. He appeared to be looking in the direction of the artist. The portrait is colored with rouge cheeks and lips so Kidd does not appear sickly. But it's possible that Mrs. Hawkins had recently tended to him and boosted his spirits.

Kidd was finally brought to trial in the Old Bailey. Led by guards and likely chained, he walked the short distance from Newgate to the adjoining building housing the courtrooms. In the distance he could see the magnificent dome of St. Paul's Cathedral. If Sarah had been in London, she would have been inside St. Paul's praying that her husband would be found not guilty.

Inside the courtroom, the accused stood at "the bar" (or in "the dock") directly facing the witness box where the prosecution and defense witnesses testified.[6] The wigged judges in their robes were seated on the other side of the room. A mirrored reflector was placed above the bar to reflect light from the windows allowing everyone present to read the expressions of the accused to assess the validity of their testimony. A sounding board was placed over their heads to amplify their voices so that every hesitation, gasp, sigh, or shout was heard. The jurors sat on the sides of the courtroom with the accused seated in the middle. At a table below where the judges sat were the clerks, lawyers, and writers who took shorthand notes that formed the proceedings. For Kidd's high-profile case, the proceedings were published in a document entitled *The Arraignment, Tryal and Condemnation of Captain William Kidd, for Murther and Piracy.*

Kidd was wearing the same suit he wore in the portrait by Sir James Thornhill. He listened carefully as he was told about his two trials, one for the murder of his crewman William Moore and the other involving the charges against him and nine of his crewmen, Nicholas Churchill, James Howe, Robert Lamley, William Jenkins, Gabriel Loff, Hugh Parrot, Richard Barleycorn, Abel Owen, and Darby Mullins for piracy. The trials lasted two days, Thursday, May 8, and Friday, May 9, 1701. Kidd's cases were highly sensationalized and newspaper reports and letters of the time show keen interest on both sides of the Atlantic. Robert Livingston followed the events closely from his vast manor in upstate New York, receiving detailed letters from informed sources including Duncan Campbell.[7] James Graham's letter calmed Livingston's fears about his involvement with Kidd, reporting that the pirate would be tried, but that he would not drag down the other investors in the *Adventure Galley* scheme. "Banish all uneasiness from [your] bosom," he wrote.[8]

How much Sarah knew is unclear: she was in New York, drawing comfort from friends and family, but it is very possible that Robert Livingston or others filled her in on what they knew, when they knew it. Livingston learned, for example, that Parliament had scrutinized the details of Kidd's commission and had previously spent five days questioning Lord Bellomont regarding his involvement. Though ultimately Bellomont was cleared of any wrongdoing "by a great majority with a great deal of honnour."[9]

Sarah's whole life was riding on the outcome of the trial. Besides the unquestionable horror of losing her husband, she was at risk of losing the property Kidd put up as collateral for his £10,000 loan from Bellomont and Livingston. Sarah never thought Kidd would have to repay the loan. She believed her husband when he said that he had not intentionally meant to harm the gunner on the *Adventure Galley*, William Moore—it was an accident that happened while he was quelling a mutiny. The French Passes, she was certain, proved he had not committed piracy. Kidd must be innocent of all the dastardly charges against him—it was his crew that was to blame for the piratical activities that took place in the Indian Ocean. For now, however, there was nothing Sarah could do but wait and hope that the king's proclamation[10] issued in March promising to pardon pirates included Kidd and that he would be freed. The king's pardon was intended to be a sweeping and efficient way to end piracy. The pardon spared pirates prosecution if they turned themselves in and promised to end their evil ways. As it turned out, Kidd was one of the pirates specifically *not* included in the king's pardon.

The fifty-six-year-old Scotsman put up a hard fight defending himself at trial and presenting to the Admiralty Court numerous documents he had written explaining why he had done what he had done and contradicting the accusations against him. Kidd wrote to the lords justices:[11]

> My Lord
> Before I made any answer to ye indictment read against me, I crave have to acquaint your Lordship that I took no ships but such as had French passes for my justification.
> In confidence that they would and ought to be allowed for my defense, I surrendered my passes to my Lord Bellomont whom I could have honored myself in favorable parts of ye world.
> But my Lord Bellomont having sold his share in my ship, and in ye Adventure, thought it his interest to make me a pirate, whereby he could claim a share of my cargo, and in order to inscript me of ye French passes, frightened & wheedled some of my men to misrepresent me and by his letters to his friend here [London] advised them to admit me a pyrate, and to obtain a new Grant of my cargo from ye King...

The letter goes on and Kidd tries to turn the case against his merchant backers: "If ye design I was set upon be illegal...my owners, who knew ye laws, ought to suffer for it, and not I, whom they made ye tool of their covetousness." Kidd realizes his demise is meant to save political careers:

"some Great men should have me dye for salving their Honour and others to pacify ye Mogull [Shah Aurangzeb] for injurys done by other men." Kidd believes he is being made an example for Henry Avery's crimes in order to placate the East India Company. He continues by saying: "Let me have my passes, I will plead [to the indictment] presently, but without them I will not plead." Kidd closes his letter boldly: "I am not afraid to dye, but I will not be my own murderer, and if an English Court will take away my life for not pleading under the circumstances, I think my death will lend very little to the credit of their justices."

Kidd's mutinous crewmen, Joseph Palmer and Robert Bradinham, testified against him. Kidd attacked their credibility with charges of perjury and mutiny: "I am sure you never heard me say such a word to such a Logger-head as you… Because I would not turn Pirate, you Rogues, you would make me one." Kidd grew indignant toward Bradinham who he accused of lying to save his own skin. "Bradinham, are not you promised your Life, to take away mine?"

Kidd had one witness, Colonel Hewson, whom he knew from fighting the French in the West Indies. The colonel gave him a glowing report saying Kidd "fought as well as any Man he ever saw."[12] But the court was not impressed because Kidd's engagement with Hewson was many years before the facts of the trial. The best witnesses for his defense were those members of his crew who were also being tried. They chose not to speak because they were jointly accused with him. Kidd was found guilty of two crimes: murdering his crewman, William Moore, and piracy. Of the nine accused crewmen, the three indentured servants—Richard Barley-corn, Robert Lamley, and William Jenkins—were cleared of charges; six others, Nicholas Churchill, James Howe, Darby Mullins, Hugh Parrot, and Gabriel Loff were found guilty. The sentence was read on May 10, 1701:[13]

> You shall be taken from the Place where you are, and be carried to the Place from whence you came, and from thence to the Place of Execution, and there be sever-ally hanged by your Necks until you be dead. And the Lord have Mercy on your Souls.

Kidd reacted loudly to the sentence, breaking the usual decorum of the chamber: "My Lord it is a very hard Sen-tence. For my Part, I am the innocentest Person of them all, only I have been sworn by Perjured Persons."[14]

The duty of the chaplain at Newgate, the reverend Paul Lorraine, was to bring Kidd to repentance. He had two weeks before the execution, scheduled for the morning of May 23, 1701, at Execution Dock on the River Thames in London. Lorraine reported that Kidd acknowledged his sins in general but he refused to admit to the charges brought against him—murder and piracy. Lorraine had spent a great deal of time with Kidd during his year of incarceration and he felt he knew him well. So well he turned his insider sta-tus into a moneymaking pamphlet and published it imme-diately after Kidd's death to satisfy the public's gruesome curiosity. In *The Ordinary of Newgate his Account of the Be-havior Confessions and Dying Words of Captain William Kidd;*

and other Pirates that were Executed at the Execution Dock in Wapping, on Friday, May 23, 1701 he wrote:[15]

> Tis true he spake some words expressing his confidence in God's mercy thro' Christ, and likewise declared that he died in charity with the world, but still I suspected his sincerity, because he was more reflective upon others than upon himself, and still would endeavour to lay his faults upon his crew and others, going about to excuse and justify himself, much about the same manner as he did when upon his trial.

He also reported that just moments before Kidd was hanged, while his former Whig patrons looked on, he proclaimed his innocence and told all those around him to send his love to his wife and daughters in New York. His greatest regret, he said, "was the thought of his wife's sorrow at his shameful death."

Hundreds gathered in a carnivalesque atmosphere to watch the event. Vendors sold food to the crowd of onlookers; spectators in boats circled near the dock to get a good look. Kidd and his accused crewmen were taken to the wooden platforms. After he'd been tied up on the gallows, the rope broke, and he fell to the ground. Disoriented but still alive, he was tied up again, even though it was illegal to hang someone twice. This time, the rope held. Admiralty tradition required that Kidd's body be left between the high and low water marks for three tides. Because he was made a special example, after his remains were cut down, his corpse was dipped in pitch and taken about twenty-five miles down the river to Tilbury Point on the Essex side of the Thames to hang in chains that kept the corpse in human form. Bodies of executed pirates were often hung from a wooden frame called a gibbet to warn others not to repeat their crimes. The corpse was chained into an iron cage to prevent relatives from taking it down and burying it. Kidd, as the condemned man, was measured for his gibbet chains by a blacksmith before his execution. This experience must have been terrifying and deeply depressing for him. He knew where his body was going to end up; he saw it, felt the cold hard metal against his skin while he practiced being dead while he was alive. Pirates were said to fear this even more than the hanging. Kidd's body was hung in the gibbet chains for many years as a gruesome warning to mariners contemplating turning pirate.[16]

26

Tragic News

Sarah did not learn of Kidd's fate immediately; news from London came by ship and the trip across the Atlantic took several weeks at least. While she waited for any news about her husband, the colonists also waited to learn who the king would appoint to be the next governor to replace Bellomont.

Sarah remained hopeful. She thought for sure Captain Winn of His Majesty's Royal Navy would bring Kidd home to her and they would return to their life on Pearl Street. With his reputation restored, she could move forward and hope association as a pirate's wife would be forgotten.

There is no record of where Sarah was, or who she was with, when she received the devastating news from London informing her that she had gone from a wife to a widow for the third time. May 16 marked their ten-year wedding anniversary and, on that day, when she and Kidd attended the hanging of the self-appointed Governor Jacob Leisler and his son-in-law, Jacob Milborne, she never imagined that their fate would become her husband's. Soon after Kidd's execution, several published accounts of the trial proceedings reached a wide audience eager for printed news about the drama that had played out on both sides of the Atlantic. It is very possible Sarah saw the publications and learned the heart-wrenching details of Kidd's attempts to save himself. She, of course, had cause to be bitter. Men she trusted—Bellomont, Duncan Campbell, and all of Kidd's investors—had betrayed her.

Many legal experts (at the time, and now) believe the evidence was insufficient to convict Kidd. He was denied witnesses and proper legal counsel and his French Passes went missing. He stood before the Admiralty Court a broken man, physically, emotionally, and mentally having endured eight months in solitary confinement in Boston followed by a year in chains in Newgate. Others believe he was caught in the middle of the political warfare between the Tories and the Whigs. The Tories called the Junto "a corporation of pirates" and demanded their dismissal. When that didn't happen, the Whigs used Kidd as a political scapegoat to save the reputations of his prominent sponsors. He was also used to appease the angry Great Mogul to show England's strong stand against men who rob at sea. If this was the case, Sarah had many more names to add to her list of betrayers.

In August 1701, Sarah received a warrant for the confiscation of Kidd's estate. She was forced to leave her home at 119–121 Pearl Street and all her household furniture and goods were seized in addition to her other properties. Due to a business arrangement with Kidd, Robert Livingston acquired 86–90 Pearl Street. To add insult to her heartache, she learned that the new attorney general assigned to New York, Sampson Broughton, wrote to the Crown and asked if he could live in one of Kidd's properties because housing was scarce and he had a large family of eight.[1]

Sarah's situation was unprecedented. At the time, she was the only woman living in Manhattan whose husband had been tried, convicted, and executed for piracy. The records make clear that a convicted pirate's actions directly affected his wife and family. The Kidd name, once the proud badge of honor of a war hero, was now tainted and those that had it were marked like a scarlet letter. For Sarah, her initials "SK" were a constant reminder that she was a pirate's wife, and her daughters, ages nine and seven years old, carried the harsh stigma of having a father shamefully remembered. Once a New York socialite, Sarah was now financially destroyed and cast adrift. The light from the candles in the brass, pewter, and tin candlesticks that illuminated her happy life with Kidd in their Pearl Street mansion were now dark.

One of the great ironies of Sarah's situation is that despite her and Kidd's best efforts to safeguard their future and safety, their many plans failed. Sarah's tragic downfall was through no fault of her own. Kidd's behavior was challenged and twisted on his voyage and the decisions he made—and some that were made for him by his mutinous crew—took him out of his customary role of captain of a privateering vessel. Sarah remained unfailingly loyal to the man she so deeply loved and believed in.

To make matters worse, Kidd's inglorious end had already transformed into folklore. The ballad "Ye Lamentable Ballad of Captain Kidd" originated in England immediately after his death in 1701. The twenty-five-verse account of Kidd's misdeeds and exploits was set to music and became wildly popular on both sides of the Atlantic. There is little doubt that Sarah heard it, and her children, too, who were old enough to understand that what was entertaining for some, was heartbreaking for others. A few verses shed light on what Sarah and the children heard. Kidd is incorrectly identified as Robert:[2]

Ye Lamentable Ballad of Captain Kidd
You captains, brave and bold, hear our cries, hear our cries,
You captains brave and bold, hear our cries,
You captains brave and bold, though you seem uncontroul'd,
Don't for the sake of gold lose your souls, lose your souls,
Don't for the sake of gold lose your souls.

My name was Robert Kidd [sic], when I sail'd, when I sail'd,
My name was Robert Kidd, when I sail'd,
My name was Robert Kidd, God's laws I did forbid,
And so wickedly I did, when I sail'd.

My parents taught me well, when I sail'd, when I sail'd,
My parents taught me well, when I sail'd,
My parents taught me well to shun the gates of hell,
But against them I did rebel, when I sail'd.

I curs'd my father dear, when I sail'd, when I sail'd,
I curs'd my father dear, when I sail'd,

I curs'd my father dear, and her that did me bear,
And so wickedly did sware, when I sail'd....

I murdered William Moore,
As I sailed, as I sailed.
I murdered William Moore,
As I sailed.
I murdered William Moore,
And I left him in his gore,
Not many leagues from shore,
As I sailed....

Come all ye young and old, see me die, see me die,
Come all ye young and old, see me die, see me die;
Come all ye young and old, you're welcome to my gold,
For by it I've lost my soul, and I must die.

Take warning now by me, for I must die, for I must die,
Take warning now by me, for I must die;
Take warning now by me, and shun bad company,
Lest you come to hell with me, for I must die,
Lest you come to hell with me, for I must die.

Sarah moved with her children to the east side of Manhattan in the East Ward and lived in strict seclusion. For two years she grieved for Kidd, longer than any of her other husbands. The census counted 4,375 white residents and between 600 and 700 Black residents in Manhattan in 1703 and Sarah was described simply as "Kidd, widd, [for widow], no head of household, two females, no slaves."[3] The ten-word sentence reveals that she was living alone with her two children and her enslaved workers and servants were taken from her with her property and furnishings. (Elizabeth Morris's four-year commitment as an indentured servant expired while Sarah was in Boston. She was promised a "double set of apparel" at the end of her contract. Sarah was in dire straits by then and it's doubtful she could have fulfilled that promise. Elizabeth Morris likely returned to New York with Sarah to collect some form of compensation.)

Her situation was made worse by the death of her brother Samuel Jr. After recovering from the shipboard illness in St. Thomas, Samuel returned to Manhattan and died without heirs. Sarah was granted the administration of his will on April 13, 1703, making her the sole beneficiary of his estate.[4] At the time of his death, he owned three properties in Manhattan: 6 Dock Street, a property on Wall Street, and one on King Street.[5] Sarah had already lost Henry who also died without heirs for his Sawkill Farm property. Cox's will specifically said that if Henry or Samuel died without issue (children), Sarah would inherit the properties he gave them.[6]

Sarah did not give up trying to restore her assets, despite her diminished situation. Her old friend, James Emott, lived in the East Ward, too, and may have helped her argue her case to the authorities that the seized properties and household furnishings were not Captain Kidd's, they were hers from her inheritance from Cox.

While her legal battles dragged through the courts, it is difficult to know how Sarah survived during this trying time. She had £160 when she was in Boston plus the six gold bars she received from Andrew Knott. Presumably she

used much of that during her many months in Boston to pay
for food, the attorney, the inn, any additional expenses, and
"tokens" she may have given to try to get Kidd free. Perhaps
Thomas Paine gave her the additional money he was hiding for her: Bellomont said at the time that he felt certain
that Paine had "a great deal more of Kidd's goods still in
his hands."[7] Rumor had it that more of Kidd's treasure remained buried on Long Island at Hempstead Harbor and off
the Connecticut coast on the Charles and Thimble Islands.[8]
But as we know, these were just rumors because only Sarah
knew the exact location of Kidd's treasure. Even if she'd
wanted to, it would have been difficult for Sarah to safely
retrieve it (with the support of the pirate network) because
her sudden income would draw attention and likely be confiscated as Kidd's assets along with her other seized goods.

Finding charity from a traditional source, like Trinity
Church, may not have been easy because of the stickiness
of her situation. Alms were dependent on the contributions
of parishioners, and even though Sarah and Kidd had been
generous benefactors—Sarah sold property to help pay for
needed acquisitions during the church's construction—she
now was damaged goods. If she did receive charity from her
spiritual home, the payment is lost to history because the
church's records from that time were destroyed in a fire in
the eighteenth century.[9] What is most probable is that Sarah's
father, an elderly man by then, and her only surviving male
relative, made sure that Sarah and his only grandchildren
did not starve. There is no written record of how Captain
Bradley felt about his son-in-law Kidd or his daughter's col-
laboration with him on a pirate ship. One can only imagine

a father's concern over his daughter's imprisonment in Boston and her now desperate situation.

With no mother to comfort her, or guidebook to advise her on the indelicate and difficult situation of being a social outcast, Sarah turned to her elderly father for more than sustenance. If there is one thing Captain Bradley understood all too well, it was the importance of a "head of household" for his daughter, especially a woman in Sarah's circumstance. A new name and a new identity would restore Sarah to her "lovely and accomplished" self. Captain Bradley set in motion a plan.

27

New Beginnings

How and when Sarah met Christopher Rousby is not clear, but it is likely that Captain Bradley had something to do with it. Rousby, Sarah's Sawkill Farm neighbor, was an East Jersey merchant living in New York, a bachelor, and on February 1, 1703, he purchased the adjoining nineteen-acre parcel that was the other half of the Riker and Lawrence Tract.[1]

Sarah inherited Sawkill Farm from her brother Henry but there were difficulties on the title. Henry died while Kidd was still alive and because of the law of coverture preventing Sarah from owning property, the deed was in Kidd's name. With Kidd's conviction as a pirate, the title was encumbered.

Captain Bradley was well aware of the legal roadblock on the property. On September 14, 1703, Sarah transferred the title to Sawkill Farm to him.[2] With the deed in Bradley's name, the integrity of the title was restored.

Sarah and Rousby spent time together at Sawkill. Henry likely maintained the farm just as Cox had left it. Horses, vegetable gardens, the grist mill, buttery, and homestead. Rousby and Sarah may have gone horseback riding down the path to the city or walked along Sawkill Creek. Rousby saw in Sarah a beautiful woman and devoted mother who had been to hell and back. He didn't have to ask her details about the Kidd ordeal, it was public knowledge printed in every newspaper in the land and across the ocean. He could even read Kidd's last dying words conveying his love for Sarah and the regret he felt for her sorrow at his shameful death.

A pirate's love for his wife is alluring and mysterious. Stolen gold, silver, jewels...on the run from the law, captured, in prison, then released and fighting for her husband's life, bribing a royal naval officer. And a baby conceived in the wild passion of it all. It is a life that Rousby, as an East Jersey merchant, could never have imagined. Sarah's experience had been frightening, and painful but fascinating all at once. And here she was, a celebrity of sorts, right in front of him. Rousby quickly learned that beneath her hardened core and keen survival instincts she was lovely.

Rousby and Sarah began to think of a future together. His land plus Sawkill Farm would restore the entire 38¼-acre parcel making it a very valuable piece of property. They could sell it for a handsome profit. But their relationship ran deeper than economic convenience. After three marriages, some better than others, Sarah knew what compatibility and chemistry looked like. Still, this could be the answer for her: a new life, a new identity, and a new father for her daughters. Rousby would have a strong, resilient, and feisty wife, sexy in a no-nonsense way. Born in 1650 in Ryton, Shropshire, England,[3] the fifty-three-year-old bachelor Rousby was attracted to this younger woman with a storied past and the idea of becoming a stepfather to the children of a famous pirate was appealing.

Two months after Sarah transferred the property to her father, Sarah married Rousby in New York on November 4, 1703.[4] Two and a half years had passed since Kidd's death. Sarah and her daughters, Elizabeth and little Sarah, eleven and nine years old, took the Rousby name. Captain Bradley sold Sawkill Farm to Rousby, the new "head of household," for two shillings on January 7, 1704.[5]

Rousby and Sarah had one more step to finalize the land transaction. They needed a new patent issued in their names for the entire parcel. On March 23, 1704, they petitioned New York's new royal governor, the flamboyant Edward Hyde, known as Lord Cornbury.[6] Cornbury made a habit of strolling the city in female attire to the surprise and dismay of many. Robert Livingston remarked: "His dressing himself in womens Cloths Commonly [every] morning is so unaccountable that if hundred[s] of Spectators didn't dayly see him, it would be incredible."[7] Cornbury's distracting appearance did not take away from his good advice. He suggested to Sarah and Rousby that they convey the property to his cousin, Queen Anne, the new monarch who replaced King William III who died from a fall while riding his horse.[8] Four months after their marriage, on March 31, 1704, they deeded the property to Queen Anne who quickly issued them a new patent on May 2, 1704.[9] She also restored Sarah's confiscated properties and issued Sarah the title to her mansion on Pearl Street.[10] Rousby and Sarah sold the Riker and Lawrence property four months later to George Duncan on September 1, 1704, for the handsome sum of £235.[11]

With her properties restored and her new life intact, Sarah gave birth to her first son, Christopher Rousby Jr., sometime in 1704. Now a family of five, on March 6, 1705, Rousby leased from George Sydenham and his wife Elizabeth a three-hundred-acre farm for nine years (the lease could be broken in three-year increments with notice by Rousby to Sydenham) at the rate of £102 a year on "Governour Stuyvesant's Bowery." The land was in the Out Ward and once owned by the fourth (and last) Dutch director general of the colony of New Netherland, Peter Stuyvesant.[12] (Stuyvesant tried and failed to resist the English takeover of the colony in 1664 but his memory is kept alive in a school, a neighborhood in Manhattan, and several other public places named after him.) Sarah's residence included a dwelling house, barns, stables, cow houses, orchards and gardens, and two enslaved workers named John and Sampson.[13] There were 10 milk cows, 8 working horses, 10 young cattle, 170 sheep, 1 sow and her pigs, 16 geese and other fowls, 2 wagons, 1 plow, 1 harrow and 1 wood sleigh.[14] While they lived there, Rousby, a man of considerable political influence, was elected to a one-year term as "Collector" of taxes in the Bowery division of the Out Ward.[15]

In 1708, Sarah gave birth to a second son. To honor her late brother whose land brought Sarah and Rousby together, she named him Henry. With their growing family of six, Rousby and Sarah continued to live in New York until at least 1714 when Rousby was made a freeman, a position that carried with it the privilege of full political rights to vote for his elected officials.[16] Why he was not made a freeman earlier is not clear but at the age of sixty-four Rousby swore an oath of loyalty to the city repeating the words that he "Shall be Contributing to all Manner of Charges with-in this City as summons, Watches, Contributions, Taxes, Tallages, Lot and Scot, and all other Charges, bearing your Part as a Freeman Ought to do."[17] In other words, he was an active contributing citizen and as a merchant he was charged a modest fee of £3.12s (three pounds and twelve shillings) to be a member of the "corporation" as it was called—the company that ran the operations of the city.

In 1709, Sarah and Rousby had a third son, William. Sarah's choice of the name could have been in memory of Kidd because that year Sarah joined forty-seven other wives of Madagascar pirates in a petition to Queen Anne asking for mercy. In particular, they requested that their husbands and kinfolk who had been detained by the authorities receive a royal pardon, and that the wealth their husbands acquired during their piratical pursuits be returned to them because it was their only means of supporting the family. Sarah signed the petition as Sarah Rousby with her mark.

The queen did not support the petition,[18] but Sarah's participation in this extraordinary document entitled "Petition of Wives and Relations of Pirats and Buckaneers of Madagascar and Elsewhere in the East and West Indies to H.M. Anne 1709"[19] showed that Sarah's memory of Kidd had not faded and that she still wished for his good name to be restored. A posthumous pardon would allow Sarah and her daughters to have a dignified end to a tragic story.

Sarah's participation also makes clear that she felt entitled to Kidd's portion of the loot. Under the terms of the articles Kidd signed with his privateering crew, he would receive thirty-five shares of the profits after the investors were paid. But whatever Kidd legally earned on the privateering voyage got forfeited after his pirate conviction. Kidd's effects, valued at £6,472, went directly to the Crown and were used to fund the Greenwich Royal Hospital and what is now the National Maritime Museum in Greenwich, England.[20]

The petition also revealed that Sarah remained active in the community of women seeking relief from their extraordinary circumstances. While there were clear-cut laws about what to do with pirates, the laws were ambiguous or nonexistent about what to do with a pirate's family because the colonial authorities did not acknowledge them.

Sarah would be reminded of her plight in a groundbreaking book on pirates that was published in London in 1724 by an anonymous source who called himself Captain Charles Johnson. *A General History of the Robberies and Murders of the Most Notorious Pyrates* was the first primary source book on pirates and it was thought at the time—and many contemporary pirate enthusiasts and scholars still consider it to be—a comprehensive and accurate account of the pirates.[21] *A General History of the Pyrates* is a two-volume, 650-page book detailing in thirty-two chapters the biographies of the "actions of a parcel of robbers" whom Captain Johnson described as "convict goal-birds or riotous persons, rotten before they are sent forth, and at best idel and only fit for the mines."[22] Johnson claimed he produced the profiles of the thirty-two pirate leaders by reading pamphlets, transcripts from pirate trials, and contemporary newspapers such as the *London Gazette* and the *Daily Post*. He also claimed he interviewed victims of the pirates or the pirates themselves. This information led him to conclude that his pirate subject was so disgusting and dishonest he would return to piracy "like the dog to the vomit"[23] after he accepted the king's pardon.

But many of the sources Johnson used were inaccurate, confusing, or contradictory. Important information contained in the eighteenth-century print literature that he used went to London by way of "merchants' letters, private communications to the trading companies' officials, reports to government boards, and reprinting of the news from colonial newspapers."[24] All too often, the transmission of this information was "second and third hand and was garbled and distorted,"[25] wrote the editor, Manuel Schonhorn. Captain Johnson also relied heavily on newspaper articles that were factually unsubstantiated and biased in favor of the authorities' position.

From the 1660s through 1730, newspapers reported the "wicked and vicious"[26] lives of the pirates to readers who were both fascinated and fearful of them. Politicians, literary men, ship owners, and merchants gathered regularly at coffeehouses around London to read the latest news of pirate activities. Little did they know that the newspapers were allied with the colonial authorities—the government published many of the newspapers or the publishers were dependent on the subsidies of the government or political parties,[27] making the reporting slanted. Other difficulties in the reporting of the pirates' activities arose because of the logistics of reporting on people and places very far away. The ocean was the pirates' workplace, and since their crimes were carried out in places "remote and solitary,"[28] it was nearly impossible for anyone to know what really happened at sea. Reports of their exploits could take weeks, months, or even years to reach land. The lag time allowed details to be forgotten or exaggerated, and because the stories were reported from secondhand or multiple sources instead of by a single credible eyewitness, the editors and publishers used the disclaimer "we have heard from..."[29] or "we are inform'd..."[30] For decades, gossip and unsubstantiated facts about pirates filled the hundreds and thousands of entries in the newspapers.[31]

From these tainted sources, Johnson created profiles of the most notorious pirates of the day, including Kidd. Schonhorn concluded that Johnson "organized, rearranged and heightened the records" of pirates and that several times there was a "reweaving" of the facts.[32]

For poor Sarah, this meant revisiting a horrible chapter in her past. *A General History of the Pyrates* was the first primary source book on pirates, and its bias against them significantly influenced popular opinion in the English public and the colonies. Many historians and pirate enthusiasts still trust the book as *the* source on eighteenth-century pirates and claim that Johnson's reporting is accurate. But Johnson's overall portrait of Kidd needs to be viewed more skeptically as a conduit of colonial authorities' propaganda, not an unimpeachable source of accurate and verifiable information.

In the twelve-page chapter on Kidd, Johnson included the painting made by Sir James Thornhill and a reprint of the king's commission assigning him the task of pirate hunter. It briefly details his voyage and trial and although he claims to give details of Kidd's life, he omits any mention of Sarah. He overlooks the important fact that Kidd was a family man with a wife and children in New York. Worse, Johnson did not interview Sarah or people who knew her. She was fifty-four years old, in good health and easily accessible in New York if he had wanted to include her perspective. The re-hash of Kidd's story had to be a setback for Sarah. Twenty-three years had passed since Kidd's death and the book no doubt brought it all back. She had five children who likely read it and for Kidd's daughters especially, it had to be hor-rendous knowing their father's image and story were forever tarnished in history. *A General History of the Pyrates* is still in print to this day, three hundred years later. For Sarah, there was no escaping Kidd's legacy.

To compound Sarah's anxiety, Rousby ran into financial and legal problems around this time. Rousby was an elderly man now, well into his seventies, and while the details of his financial problems are not known, it's unlikely that the publication of *A General History of the Pyrates* was related to his inability to pay the rent of £102 a year to George Syden-ham and his wife, Elizabeth, for the farm in the Bowery. He moved Sarah and the family out of New York to a small, less expensive farm that he leased in Rahway, New Jersey, about twenty-one miles southwest of Manhattan. Primarily a Quaker community, Rahway was in the bounds of Eliz-abeth Town in Essex County (today Rahway is in Union County). Sydenham sued Rousby for the money and on De-cember 14, 1727, Rousby was issued a £150 bail bond.[33] The only surviving document from the case is a sworn statement from Rousby stating that he was unaware of the trial date and did not have time to subpoena his main witness, Gabriel Ludlow, a clerk of the New York Assembly.

Rousby and Sarah had been married nearly a quarter of a

century, longer than any of her other marriages combined. Her five children ranged in ages from about thirty-four to seventeen. It is not known how the lawsuit concluded, there are no records of the outcome in the primary sources, but it had to have been embarrassing for Sarah and a disturbing disruption for the children.

Christopher Rousby died ten months later at the age of seventy-eight on October 31, 1728.[34] The cause of death is not listed on the death notice but given that his will was hastily written on October 3 when he was "weak and sick in body but of sound and perfect mind and memory" it may have been from old age exacerbated by the stress of his financial difficulties. He empowered "his beloved wife, Sarah, to have full power and absolute authority" over his real and personal estate.[35]

Inventories were usually taken after a death, but Rousby's was made three days before he died, suggesting that when he became gravely ill, Sarah began making the necessary arrangements to list the material possessions of their long marriage. The inventory of Rousby's estate was valued at £110, just a little more than the yearly rent of £102 for the Bowery. It is in sharp contrast to Cox's £1900, and offers us a window into Sarah's life at the time.[36]

The details show that the Rousbys lived with their four children—Elizabeth, Christopher, Henry, and William—and two enslaved workers, "an old man and a young negro woman."[37] Young Sarah was married and lived in New York with her husband, Joseph Latham, a shipwright. Latham was more than just a carpenter or woodworker, he had the expertise to find among the collection of old scraps of wood the perfect piece to cut, sand, shape, and fit into a vessel that had to be watertight and seaworthy.[38] A shipwright was a sought-after artisan and the Lathams lived near his workplace at a shipyard near the water.

Rousby owned fourteen "old" books,[39] a significant number for the time. There were horses (two old ones, a year-old mare and a mare with a colt), three cows, seven pigs, and sixteen sheep. They grew wheat, rye, oats, and corn; made butter and cheese; and the women spun the wool shorn from the sheep on two spinning wheels. Two pairs of curtains hung in the windows—one made of calico; two rugs (one homespun) adorned their floors. One bed—probably Sarah and Rousby's—had a bolster and pillow. There was a hammock to rest in, a couch and six pairs of chairs to sit on, and a cradle left over from when the children were babies. It is almost certain that "one and a half pairs of old turkey work chairs, an old table, old table frame, an old desk, an old chest of drawers, an old large looking glass and old pewter" were originally in Sarah's home on Pearl Street and were in the mansion when Sarah set up housekeeping with Kidd in 1691. That Sarah furnished her Rousby home with these repurposed items suggests that she was both a practical homemaker and that each and every item meant a great deal to her. It wouldn't be long before she returned them to their original place—Manhattan.

28

Full Circle

After Rousby's death, Sarah gave up the farm in Rahway and moved back to Manhattan with her children. She may have noticed the many changes in the colony. For one, the population had nearly doubled from the time she was counted in 1703. There were now 8,600 residents according to the census taker in 1731.[1] A map of the city from 1730 reflected the city's growing commercialism with more wharfs and new structures.[2] Trinity Church now had 178 male taxpayers and had been renovated to serve the growing needs of the community.[3] Trade with the West Indies had increased, making the city more cosmopolitan. And markets at the foot of each street along the East River and in the center of the city suggested that the colonists who once gathered their own food now relied on outside sources for their needs.[4]

Sarah learned that her son-in-law, Joseph Latham, died on May 19, 1732, leaving young Sarah a widow with small children.[5] It may have been this tragic news that shifted Sarah's focus inward to protect the needs of her children and generations to come. With the help of her lawyer, she composed her Last Will and Testament on November 1, 1732, at the age of sixty-two.[6] Of all her surviving documents, the will is the most revealing and intimate: it shows her to be, as one person who knew her reported, "a lady of intelligence & exemplary piety."[7]

At more than two pages, her will is considerably more robust than many wills of the time and much longer than the wills of her late husbands, Cox and Rousby. (Kidd and Oort did not leave wills.) Unlike Rousby whose Last Will and Testament was written at the end of his life, Sarah chose to write hers while she was still "in Good Health and of Perfect Mind & Memory."[8] Her intentions were clear and purposeful. She asked "Almighty God and to his Son Jesus Christ my savior and redeemer and to the Holy Ghost three persons and one God…to have mercy on my soul and to pardon and to forgive me all my sins & offences so that I may after this Miserable Life arise with the elect and have the life and fruition of the Godhead by the Death and passion of our savior Jesus Christ according to his Mercifull promise in that Behalf."[9]

Her commanding voice is heard in her stern instructions to her five children. It is a testament to Sarah's physical vigor and robust character that five of her children lived to adulthood. She implored that Elizabeth Troup, Sarah Latham, Christopher Jr., Henry, and William be "contented with this my Last Will and Testament without any trouble or Vexation of any of them against the other…concerning all or any part of my Estate Real or Personal as they will answer for the sins before the judgment seat of God who is the rewarder of all Good Persons and a sensere [sincere] judge and Revenger of all those that do Evil."[10]

She appointed her son Christopher Jr. and son-in-law John Troup Jr., both wigmakers, to be her executors and ordered them to "sell all my Houses, Lands Tenements and Hereditaments and apprentences Whatsoever in the City of New York or elsewhere within some convenient time after my decease and the money thereby arising to be equally Divided in Five equal parts among my five children...of all my Estate both Real and Personal."[11] She added that "During the time and till my Houses and Lands and Tenements are sold by my Executors aforesaid the Moneys arising for rent of the same after repairs and Taxes Deducted the Residue to be equally Divided among my aforesaid Five children part & part alike."[12]

It had been four years since Rousby's death, and if Sarah still owned the two enslaved people she inherited from Rousby—an older man and young woman—she would have left instructions to her heirs in her will, much like her contemporary, Catherine van Cortland Philipse, did ordering that "her slaves were to be manumitted and sett at full freedom and Liberty...one Month after my decease."[13]

Sarah noted that she had assets in "the City of New York and elsewhere." She did not identify "elsewhere." This implies there were valuables at an undisclosed location. One can only speculate if this was Kidd's treasure or something else of immense rare value.

To the everyday reader, Sarah's will is interesting but not tantalizing. Hers could be the last wishes of any wealthy New York woman who lived in the colonial period. But a closer look reveals much more. At the bottom of the last page is Sarah's signature. It is witnessed by Benjamin Hildreth, "taylor," and Abraham Vanwych, merchant. This was not the mark she put on all her other documents. Instead she wrote eleven letters—*Sarah Rousby*.[14] Sometime between 1708, when she signed the pirates' wives petition to Queen Anne with her mark, and 1732, Sarah learned to write her name. This extraordinary achievement, between the ages of thirty-eight and sixty-two, shows just how ambitious and determined she was to be more than an ordinary colonial woman. Her successful undertaking completed her transformation from "SK" to Sarah Rousby.

At the time of her writing, it had been more than three decades since she'd become a pirate's wife. She carefully crafted her will to hide her dark past, skillfully listing her daughters by their married names, Sarah Latham and Elizabeth Troup, to protect their identities. Anyone reading Sarah's will would not know that she was Sarah Kidd, widow of the notorious pirate. They would not know that she had been an accomplice to an outlaw, lived on a pirate ship, mingled with murderers, and served time in prison. Her most revealing and informative historical document belied such truths.

Sarah's secret was safe in the historical literature. In the end, the erasure of Sarah's existence in *A General History of the Pyrates* worked in her favor. And so did the fact that the Golden Age of Piracy was all but over.

The men who boldly walked the streets of Manhattan in their stolen finery, peddled their plundered loot, and filled the coffers of ladies of the night had been captured or killed. Robbery at sea had been a lucrative enterprise for many state-sanctioned plundering operations, but England's attitude toward global piracy had changed. The harsh example made of Kidd, coupled with legislation enacted in 1700 called "An Act for the more Effectual Suppression of Piracy"[15] amounted to a pirate crackdown. The authorities in London established Admiralty Courts in the colonies to more quickly and conveniently bring pirates to justice. More naval ships were out chasing sea robbers who disrupted international trade. The change was noticeable across the globe and especially in New York, the hub of North American piracy. The *New York Gazette* reported more stories containing the names of ships going in and out of Manhattan's busy seaport instead of stories about ship captures and stolen cargo by pirates.

Sarah's presence in the historical record is scant for the last twelve years of her life. Some writers have claimed that she opened a tavern and operated it for many years until her death. This is very unlikely. Operating a tavern was a massive undertaking in the eighteenth century, especially for someone like Sarah who had no experience as a tavern keeper. Many female barkeepers inherited taverns from their husbands or fathers or had a relative post the necessary bond with the mayor's office and paid a fee (not more than £10) to obtain the necessary license.[16] If Sarah had operated a tavern, there would have been a record of her license and of the taxes she was required to pay.[17] There are no such records in the historical sources.

In 1739, seven years after she wrote her will, Sarah sold one of her many properties—a house on the north side of Dock Street in Manhattan. This is likely one of the three properties she inherited from Samuel Jr. To solicit buyers, she posted an advertisement in the *New-York Weekly Journal* on October 15, 1739. Why she liquidated this property is unclear, but the names involved in the transaction suggest that she may have been giving her children an early cash installment from her estate. Her ad reads:[18]

To be sold the House and Ground now in Tenure of Mr. John Breese: The Lott contains as much in Front as both the Houses Directly opposite: And has more Depth, then any in that Block Except those that Front both Streets: Enquire of the Widdow Rousby or John Troup.

From November 1740 to March 1741, snow blanketed New York in what was remembered as the hardest winter on record. The punishing weather brought the region to a standstill. New York harbor was frozen for six weeks, a rare occurrence given that it was salt water and had never been known to freeze. Ships were locked out, preventing much-needed supplies from coming into the colony. The *New-York Weekly Journal* reported on December 22, "Our Streets are fill'd with Heaps of Snow,"[19] referring to the shoulder-deep drifts on the cobblestone that hindered carriages, horses, and pedestrians. Then came a series of northeasters that pounded the eastern colony with howling winds, sleet, and ice. The whole area had frozen so solid that a future signer of the Declaration of Independence, Francis Lewis, rode a sleigh two hundred miles from Barnstable on Cape Cod, Massachusetts, to New York City along the Atlantic's shoreline.[20] Residents were homebound in poorly heated houses because wood and coal were hard to come by. The situation grew more dire when war broke out between England and Spain. As food grew scarce, anxiety increased, especially among the poor and the nearly two thousand enslaved men, women, and their children.[21]

Later in March 1741, fire broke out at the southern end of Manhattan. Flames spread from the governor's mansion in the fort. Lieutenant Governor George Clark tried to stop the blazes from going up Broadway, the hundred-foot-wide thoroughfare, to the city's tall wooden buildings. The secretary's office housed a valuable collection of documents, including the governor's papers, official commissions, private letters, newspapers, and council records, but they were not able to be saved.[22] A total of ten fires broke out over a period of weeks and after much destruction, the bucket brigades and fire engines put out the flames.

Emotions ran high and on April 11, 1741, the Common Council convened to try to figure out who or what had caused the destruction. The alderman carried out a search of each house in his ward, looking for suspicious characters.[23] Sarah's house in the East Ward, and those of her children, were searched.

Rumors spread that a group of enslaved and free Black New Yorkers and some poor white settlers set the fires in what came to be known as the "Great Negro Plot" of 1741. Their alleged plan was to seize the town, murder people in power, and set up a government of their own. The conspiracy led to mass hysteria and violence, which lasted from May to August.[24]

A month or so before the fires, in a seemingly unrelated incident, three enslaved people robbed a small store owned by a white couple. One of the robbers, Caesar, brought his booty to a dockside tavern owned by a poor and illiterate cobbler named John Hughson known for dealing with stolen goods. His tavern was a favorite meeting place of young men who enjoyed after-hours carousing. His tavern offered lodging and was the residence of a sex worker with many names, but lastly, Peggy Kerry, who was described as the Newfoundland Irish beauty "of the worst sort."[25] (She'd recently had a child by Caesar.) Caesar and one of his partners in the robbery, Prince, were arrested.

A judge appointed to lead the investigation and preside over the trials, Daniel Horsmanden, was anxious to connect the fires and the robbery. A jury was assembled on April 21, 1741, and a sixteen-year-old indentured servant at Hughson's tavern, Mary Burton, was called to testify. In exchange for her cooperation she would be freed from her indenture. Seeing this as her road to freedom, she testified that three enslaved workers, Caesar, Prince, and Cuffee (seen running away from the fire at the fort), along with a group of poor white settlers had plotted to burn the fort and the city and kill its inhabitants. She also implicated Peggy Kerry. Kerry was forced to testify and implicated many Blacks in the conspiracy, and on the basis of her testimony, those she named were put in custody in the dungeon below City Hall. Those in custody were also forced to testify and name names.

In May, Caesar and Prince were hanged not for conspiracy but for burglary. Peggy Kerry, Hughson, and his wife were arrested and found guilty of receiving stolen goods and hanged. Horsmanden, eager for any information, offered rewards in varying amounts to anyone coming forward with information about the fires: £100 to whites, £45 to free Blacks or Indigenous people, and £20 plus freedom to enslaved people.[26]

Burton continued her accusations and more than twenty white people, including a Catholic Latin teacher named John Ury, were accused of participating in the rebellion. Horsmanden summoned all the town's lawyers to assist the attorney general with the prosecution of over 150 people. The defendants were denied legal counsel and many of the accused, poor and uneducated without a clear understanding of the situation, were led to believe they would be pardoned and confessed.[27] Of the 154 enslaved and free Black New Yorkers arrested, more than half confessed to conspiring to destroy the city.[28] Fourteen were burned at the stake, eighteen hanged, seventy-one deported and the rest pardoned or discharged for want of proof.[29] Twenty white people were committed to prison and four of them were executed.[30]

Rumors, false accusations, and finger-pointing aided the belief that the plot actually existed, leading to the horrific deaths, exile, and imprisonment of many. While an official conspiracy was not proven, this event shows the immense racial and socioeconomic tensions of the era.

Sarah must have watched the events carefully. If she still owned enslaved people, hers were not involved or implicated.[31] But she certainly knew enslaved people that were. Cuffee belonged to Frederick Philipse's son, Adolph; he confessed to setting fire to the fort and was burned at the stake.[32] And one of Frederick Philipse's 210 enslaved workers was involved but discharged. Some white New Yorkers attended the horrid events watching Black people burn at the stake and hang on the gallows.[33] Sarah's neighbor, Elizabeth DeLancy, attended the executions and wrote to her father, Stephen DeLancy, a prominent merchant, that "The chief talk now in Town is about the negroes conspiracy."[34] These gruesome public executions may have reminded Sarah of the carnival-like atmosphere reported in letters and literature about onlookers who attended Kidd's hanging. Or her own attendance on her wedding day to Kidd of the hanging of Jacob Leisler and Jacob Milborne.

Soon, a citizens' watch was established to patrol and protect the community against future uprisings.[35] Every able-bodied man was required to take his turn on duty and Sarah's sons were required to participate.

In the middle of July 1743, an epidemic of yellow fever broke out in Manhattan taking 217 lives in two months.[36] It was the fourth outbreak since 1702 and still no one knew how to cure the deadly disease transmitted by a mosquito that produced fever followed by chills, yellowing of the skin, and bloody vomiting.[37] Sarah Kidd Latham, Sarah's younger daughter, may have been one of the victims of yellow fever when she died on August 6, 1743, at the age of forty-nine. The news of her daughter's death must have been wrenching for Sarah. She went to her daughter's home near the shipyard to be with her grandchildren. Seeing her deceased daughter may have brought back heartbreaking memories of the trauma little Sarah experienced as a seven-year-old, when both her parents were imprisoned in Boston, and a ship took Kidd away to London.

That memory and others made her determined to protect

her daughter's children. She couldn't shield her own daughters from those horrific events, but she could make sure her grandchildren had money to survive. Just hours after her daughter's death, Sarah contacted her lawyer and gathered witnesses to add a codicil to her will.[38] In two sentences she protected the interests of young Sarah's children to ensure they would receive a share of her estate. She confidently signed her full name again, Sarah Rousby.

Sometime over the next thirteen months, another tragedy struck. Christopher Jr. died at the age of about forty. For someone who paid such fastidious attention to her records, it's telling that Sarah never updated her will to reflect the loss. She had bequeathed her gold wedding band to Christopher Jr., and it remained in his name.[39] She was too grief-stricken to attend to such a trivial detail.

Fortune finally brought happy news in March 1744, when Henry Rousby, a shipwright, and his wife, Emma, had their second child, a baby boy. Following in the family tradition of naming a child after a loved one, they chose Christopher, after Henry's father and recently deceased brother. They named their other child, a daughter, Sarah after her grandmother and recently deceased aunt. It is likely Sarah would have known she was going to have another grandchild and may have participated in the birth with her daughter-in-law, Emma, as was the custom of the time. Sarah may have helped her make "groaning cake" or assisted with serving "groaning beer" to the ladies in attendance for the birth.

A few months later, a diphtheria outbreak raged through New York and the eastern colonies of Massachusetts and

New Hampshire.[40] The epidemic hit Sarah's family especially hard. Within months, three generations of Sarah's family would be lost. Sarah died on Saturday, September 12, 1744. Four months later, her son Henry, and his ten-month-old baby, Christopher, died on the same day, January 25, 1745.[41] They are all buried together in the churchyard of Trinity Church Wall Street in Manhattan.

With the death of her son Christopher, the inventory of Sarah's estate was taken by the other executor, John Troup Jr. Unfortunately, the detailed assessment of Sarah's land and personal property has not survived in the historical records.[42] It would be important to know if Sarah kept among her personal belongings her most treasured possessions: the traveling trunk with the silver tankard, silver mug, silver porringer, spoons, and forks that she packed when she fled New York for Block Island to meet Kidd, or her stitchery that she brought from England. Whatever assets Sarah had at the end of her life were distributed to her daughter Elizabeth, her son William, the spouses of Henry and Christopher Jr., and the children of her daughter Sarah.

The man who brought Sarah into history was Captain Kidd. Without his notoriety as a pirate, Sarah would have remained invisible in colonial history. Her initials, "SK," scratched on a few documents give only fleeting clues into her existence. Those bold pen strokes revealed a narrative we have only imagined—the dangerous, difficult, and thrilling journey of a pirate's wife. They shed unexpected light on a young colonial woman caught up in a world of politics, passion, and grisly eighteenth-century justice.

When Sarah arrived in the New World from England in 1684, she had two names: Sarah Bradley. Over the next sixty years, she added four more: Cox, Oort, Kidd, and Rousby. Yet Sarah's legacy, shaped in part by the mother she lost and the men she loved, is uniquely her own, one spanning continents and farms and merchant shops and treasure-filled pirate ships. Her indomitable determination to survive and care for those she loved is her lasting gift. It is a gift far greater than silver and gold.

★ ★ ★ ★ ★

Acknowledgments

In writing this book on Sarah Kidd's life, I relied upon innumerable sources. I am grateful to the staff at the Library of Congress, the New York Public Library, the Massachusetts State Archives, The National Archives in London, the New England Historical Society, the Block Island Town Clerk's office and American Ancestors. I would like to thank Dr. Kimberly Alexander, Luis Alvarez, Rosemary Enright, Dr. Oliver Finnegan, Katherine Flynn, Whitey Flynn, Margaret (Maggi) Gonsalves, Dr. Lucas Haasis, Marissa Maggs and Ann McClellan for their generous help and expertise.

Thank you to the editorial, marketing, publicity and sales team at Hanover Square Press. Thank you to Quinn Banting for designing the perfect book cover. Thank you to my copyeditor, Tracy Wilson, and my publicists, Leah Morse and Lia Ferrone. A very, very special thank you to my amazing editor, John Glynn, whose enthusiasm, skill, and professionalism made the project seamless. A pleasure to work with, he made the book better in so many ways.

This book is lovingly dedicated to the memory of my

grandmother Juliette Marie Wehrmann Palmer, who lived in New Orleans, Louisiana. She, like Sarah Kidd, was fiercely devoted to those she loved.

I could not have written this book without the love and support of my family. I am immensely proud of my two daughters, Christina and Danielle Geanacopoulos, and my son-in-law, Dan Pollock. My calm and patient husband, David, remains the great blessing of my life.

Endnotes

Abbreviations:

C.O.—Colonial Office Paper

HCA—High Court of Admiralty Papers

PRO—Public Record Office

Prologue

1. Will of Sarah Rousby, *New York County, Wills and Administrations 1742-1751*, 15:262–264.

1. Sarah's New World

1. J.H. Innes, *New Amsterdam and Its People* (New York: Charles Scribner's Sons, 1902), 249.

2. Joyce Goodfriend, *Before the Melting Pot: Society and Culture in Colonial New York* (Princeton: Princeton University Press, 1994), 78.

3. George J. Lankevich, *New York City, A Short History* (New York: New York University Press, 2002), 26.

4. Morton Pennybacker, "Captain Kidd: Hung, Not for Piracy but for Causing the Death of a Rebellious Seaman Hit with a Toy Bucket"

in *New York History*, vol. 25, no. 4 (October 1944), 485. Accessed March 7, 2014. http://www.jstor.org/stable/23148755.

5. Edwin G. Burrows and Mike Wallace, *Gotham: A History of New York City to 1898* (New York: Oxford University Press, 2000), 87.

6. Alice Morse Earle, *Colonial Days in Old New York* (New York: Charles Scribner's Sons, 1896; Singing Tree Press, Detroit, Michigan, 1968), 58.

7. Gideon J. Tucker, *Names of Persons for Whom Marriage Licenses were Issued by the Secretary of the Province of New York Previous to 1784* (Albany: Weed, Parsons and Company, 1860), 577; Peter R. Christoph and Florence A. Christoph., eds, *New York Historical Manuscripts: English Books of General Entries of the Colony of New York 1674-1688* (Baltimore: Genealogical Publishing Co., 1982), 325.

8. Sarah Bradley was born about 1670 in England. https://records.myheritagelibraryedition.com/research/record-1-394707701-1-25/sarah-bradl. Accessed February 7, 2019.

9. Laurel Thatcher Ulrich, *Good Wives, Image and Reality in the Lives of Women in Northern New England 1650-1750* (New York: Vintage Books, 1991), 6.

10. William Cox was granted a pass from New York governor Edmund Andros on April 16, 1676, to be a passenger on the ketch *Beginning* bound from New York to Barbados. This means he was old enough to travel on his own and lived in New York at least eight years before he met Sarah in 1684. Peter R. Christoph and Florence A. Christoph, eds., *New York Historical Manuscripts: English-Books of General Entries of the Colony of New York, 1674-1688* (Baltimore: Genealogical Publishing Co., 1982), 111–112.

11. Author interview with Hallie Borstel, researcher, New England Historic Genealogical Society, Boston, by email October 2, 2019.

12. This information taken from the inventory of William Cox.

13. Earle, *Colonial Days in Old New York*, 110.

14. This information taken from the inventory of William Cox.

15. "American Needlework in the Eighteenth Century." www.metmu-seum.org/toah/hd/need/hd_need.htm. Accessed January 15, 2022.

16. This information taken from the inventory of William Cox.

17. https://www.college-of-arms.gov.uk. Accessed February 2, 2022.

18. Earle, *Colonial Days in Old New York*, 70.

19. Ibid., 56–60.

20. Ibid., 64–65.

2. William Cox and the She-Merchant

1. David T. Valentine, *History of the City of New York* (New York: G.P. Putnam & Co., 1853), 180.

2. Lankevich, *New York City, A Short History*, 26.

3. The colony had a reputation as a flour-producing entity and the city's viability and development was dependent on the flour merchants doing their job well. The flour monopoly was so successful that the city's wealth and population tripled before the end of the seventeenth century, according to historian George J. Lankevich in *New York City, A Short History*. Flour barrels and windmills are on the seal of New York City to represent one of the city's earliest trade products and the great wealth generated by the Bolting Act.

4. William Cox and John Robinson and wife Greetje. Deed dated February 12, 1683, *Liber Deeds*, IX:3 (Albany). 13:28. "New York Land Records, 1630-1975," images, *FamilySearch* (https://family search.org/ark:/61903/3:1:3QS7-99WG-KHX4?cc=2078654 &wc=M7CX-B3N%3A358138101%2C360793801: 22 May 2014), New York > Conveyances 1654-1687 vol. 13 > image 263-264 of 431; county courthouses, New York. Accessed January 2, 2020.

5. Michael Pollak, "FYI: Name that Island," *New York Times*, December 14, 2012. https://www.nytimes.com/2012/12/16/nyregion/before-it-was-called-roosevelt-island.html. Accessed August 22, 2021.

6. Henry Croswell Tuttle, *Abstracts of Farm Titles in the City of New York, East Side, Between 75th and 120th Streets* (New York: The Spectator Company, 1878), 4.

7. https://www.newnetherlandinstitute.org/history-and-heritage/additional-resources/dutch-treats/peter-schagen-letter/. Accessed December 3, 2021. Value of the guilder/euro conversion at International Institute of Social History, www.ilsg.nl.

8. Berthold Fernow and Arnold J. F. Van Laer, *Calendar of Council Minutes 1688-1783* (Harrison, NY: Harbor Bill Books, 1987), 34.

9. The names of Cox's enslaved workers, Moll and Titus, taken from the inventory of his estate made in 1689.

10. Michelle Marchetti Coughlin, *One Colonial Woman's World: The Life and Writings of Mehetabel Chandler Coit* (Boston: University of Massachusetts Press, 2021), 27.

11. Dunbar Maury Hinrichs, *Mrs. Captain Kidd* (New York: Vantage Press, 1952), 41.

12. Zimmerman, Jean. *The Women of the House.* New York: Harcourt, 2006.

13. Carol Berkin and Leslie Horowitz, *Women's Voices, Women's Lives* (Boston: Northeastern University Press, 1998), 96.

14. "New York Land Records, 1630-1975," images, *FamilySearch* (https://familysearch.org/ark:/61903/3:1:3QS7-L9W5-G5TC?cc=2078654&wc=M7CX-B3X%3A358138101%2C360792501: 22 May 2014), New York > Conveyances 1683-1896 vol 18 > images 28-31 of 418; county courthouses, New York. Accessed January 2, 2020.

15. Innes, *New Amsterdam and Its People*, 241; Valentine, *History of the City of New York*, 178.

16. Valentine, *History of the City of New York*, 289.

17. Valentine, *History of the City of New York*, 76; Innes, *New Amsterdam and Its People*, 235.

18. "New York Land Records, 1630–1975," images, *FamilySearch* (https://familysearch.org/ark:/61903/3:1:3QS7-L9W5-G5TC?cc=2078654&wc=M7CX-B3X%3A358138101%2C360792501: 22 May 2014), New York > Conveyances 1683-1896 vol 18 > images 28-31 of 418; county courthouses, New York. Accessed January 2, 2020.

19. This information is taken from the inventory of Cox's estate from August 1689.

20. This information is taken from the inventory of Cox's estate from August 1689; explanation of where things originated from in Cathy Matson, *Merchants & Empire Trading in Colonial New York* (Baltimore: The Johns Hopkins University Press, 1998), 90.

21. Earle, *Colonial Days in Old New York*, 179.

22. Ibid., 180.

23. Zimmerman, *The Women of the House*, 237.

24. Earle, *Colonial Days in Old New York*, 292.

25. Ibid.

26. Information about Cox's business practices in the shop taken from the inventory of his estate.

27. The inventory from Cox's estate lists these people as some of his customers who bought their goods on credit.

28. Frederick de Peyster, "The Life and Administration of Richard,

Earl of Bellomont," an address delivered before the New York Historical Society, November 18, 1879 (New York: *New York Historical Society Collections*, 1879), 29.

3. Mayhem and Tragedy

1. http://www.nycourts.gov/history/legal-history-new-york/legal-history-eras-01/history-new-york-legal-eras-leisler.html. Accessed February 12, 2020; Edwin G. Burrows and Mike Wallace, *Gotham: A History of New York City to 1898* (New York: Oxford University Press, 1999), 94–95.

2. Burrows and Wallace, Gotham: *A History of New York City to 1898*, 95.

3. www.u-s-history.com/pages/h547.html. Accessed January 15, 2022.

4. Burrows and Wallace, Gotham: *A History of New York City to 1898*, 96.

5. Ibid., 98.

6. Peter R. Christoph, ed. *The Dongan Papers 1683-1688: Admiralty Court and other Records of the Administration of New York Governor Thomas Dongan* (Syracuse: Syracuse University Press, 1993), 238.

7. Joyce D. Goodfriend, *Before the Melting Pot, Society and Culture in Colonial New York City, 1664-1730* (Princeton: Princeton University Press, 1992), 61.

8. Innes, *New Amsterdam and Its People*, 249; Land record in www.FamilySearch.org, April 8, 1689, 18:97.

9. *New York: Abstracts of Wills, Admins. and Guardianships, 1787-1835.* (Online database: AmericanAncestors.org. New England Historic Genealogical Society, 2006.) Original manuscript in: Eardeley Genealogy Collection: New York State Abstracts of Wills, Brooklyn Historical Society. https://www.americanancestors.org/DB7/i/6903/679/417487).

10. Men of wealth and standing in colonial New York followed the fashion trends in Europe. www.fashionhistory.fitnyc.edu/1680-1689. Accessed December 4, 2021.

11. Innes, *New Amsterdam and Its People*, 250; E.B. O'Callaghan, ed., "Mr. Tuder to Captain Nicholson," in *Documents Relative to the Colonial History of the State of New York*, vol. 3 (Albany: Weed, Parsons, and Company, 1852-53), 617.

12. Innes, *New Amsterdam and Its People*, 250; Hinrichs, *Mrs. Captain Kidd*, 38.

13. Mariana Griswold Van Rensselaer, *History of the City of New York in the Seventeenth Century, Volume 2: New York Under the Stuarts* (New York: Cosimo Classics, 2007), 408.

14. Robert C. Ritchie, *The Duke's Province: A Study of New York Politics and Society, 1664-1691* (Chapel Hill: The University of North Carolina Press, 1977), 26.

15. Earle, *Colonial Days in Old New York*, 306.

16. Burrows and Wallace, *Gotham: A History of New York City to 1898*, 174.

17. Cathy Matson, *Merchants & Empire Trading in Colonial New York* (Baltimore: The Johns Hopkins University Press), 74.

18. "Turkey work embroidery." www.britannica.com/art/Turkey-work. Accessed January 15, 2022.

19. This information taken from the inventory of William Cox.

20. Berkin and Horowitz, *Women's Voices, Women's Lives*, 96.

21. This information is taken from the 1691 inventory of William Cox's estate appraised by Jacob Mayle and Richard Jones.

22. Zimmerman, *The Women of the House*, 184.

23.   Valentine, *History of the City of New York*, 221.

24.   Matson, *Merchants & Empire Trading in Colonial New York*, 61.

4. Debts and Bills

1.   Harold T. Wilkins, *Captain Kidd and His Skeleton Island* (New York: Liveright Publishing, 1937), 32; Dunbar Maury Hinrichs, *The Fateful Voyage of Captain Kidd* (New York: Bookman Associates, Inc., 1955), 17.

2.   Hinrichs, *The Fateful Voyage of Captain Kidd*, 19.

3.   Robert C. Ritchie, *Captain Kidd and the War Against the Pirates* (Cambridge: Harvard University Press, 1986), 30–31.

4.   Kidd referred to this in his letter to the Earl of Orford, April 11, 1700, on board HMS *Advice*, Portland MSS., British Museum. Also cited in Hinrichs, *The Fateful Voyage of Captain Kidd*, 19.

5.   https://beyond-the-shore.obsidianportal.com/wikis/ship-types. Accessed March 28, 2020.

6.   Ritchie, *Captain Kidd and the War Against the Pirates*, 32; Hinrichs, *The Fateful Voyage of Captain Kidd*, 20.

7.   Burrows and Wallace, *Gotham: A History of New York City to 1898*, 113; Wilkins, *Captain Kidd and His Skeleton Island*, 31.

8.   E.B. O'Callaghan, ed. *The Documentary History of the State of New York*, vol. 2 (Albany: Weed Parsons & Co. Public Printer, 1849), 380; Lankevich, *New York City*, 30.

9.   Hugh Hastings, *Ecclesiastical Records, State of New York*, vol. 2 (Albany: James B. Lyon, State Printer, 1901), 998.

10.   Richard Zacks, *The Pirate Hunter* (New York: Hyperion, 2002), 83.

11.   Linda Briggs Biemer, *Women and Property in Colonial New York:*

The Transition from Dutch to English Law, 1643-1727 (Ann Arbor: UMI Research Press, 1983), 1.

12. Linda Grant DePaul, *Women and the Law: The Colonial Period*, an article from a Symposium: Women and the Law, A Retrospective View, 109. HeinOnline 6 Hum.Rts.107 1976–1977. Accessed February 10, 2020.

13. Wilkins, *Captain Kidd and His Skeleton Island*, 30.

14. New York Title and Guarantee Company, *New York Land-Holding Sea Rover* (New York: Lotus Press, 1901), 1–5.

15. Burrows and Wallace, *Gotham: A History of New York City to 1898*, 124.

16. C.O. 323:2, no. 124, PRO, "Deposition of Benjamin Franks."

17. Steven Struzinski, "The Tavern in Colonial America," *The Gettysburg Historical Journal* 1, Article 7, 2002, 31. https://cupola.gettysburg.edu/ghj/vol1/iss1/7. Accessed June 1, 2021.

18. Wilkins, *Captain Kidd and His Skeleton Island*, 32; De Peyster, *The Life and Administration of Richard, Earl of Bellomont*, 32.

19. Details of Kidd taken from an anonymous portrait of him. Tradition has it that Sir James Thornhill drew Kidd when he was appearing before the House of Commons in London at the age of fifty-six. This is the only known portrait of Kidd done from real life.

5. Dead Men Tell No Tales

1. Robert Hendre Kelby and Kenneth Scott, *New York Marriages Previous to 1784* (Baltimore: Genealogical Publications Co., 1968). Kidd could not get a marriage license the same way Cox and Oort did. With so short notice he had to apply for a penal bond that showed there was no "lawful let or impediment of Pre-Contract, Affinity or Consanguinity to hinder the parties being joined in the Holy

Bonds of Matrimony and afterwards their living together as Man and Wife."

2. Gideon J. Tucker, *Names of Persons for Whom Marriage Licenses Were Issued by the Secretary of the Province of New York, Previous to 1784* (Albany: Weed, Parsons and Company, 1860), 578.

3. Burrows and Wallace, *Gotham: A History of New York City to 1898*, 102.

4. Hinrichs, *The Fateful Voyage of Captain Kidd*, 22; *Trial of Jacob Leisler, New York Historical Society Collections*, 1868; Innes, *New Amsterdam and Its People*, 247.

5. Innes, *New Amsterdam and Its People*, 247.

6. Administration of the Estate of John Oort in *Abstracts of Wills on File in the Surrogate's Office, City of New York, 1665-1801*, 1:180, 1:183.

7. This information is taken from the inventory of John Oort's estate done by Captain William Kidd and Sarah Kidd, October 17, 1692, found in Kenneth Scott and James A. Owre, *Genealogical Data from Data from Inventory of New York Estates 1666-1825* (New York: New York Genealogical and Biographical Society, 1970), 110.

8. Earle, *Colonial Days in Old New York*, 102–103.

9. Ibid., 108.

10. Zacks, *The Pirate Hunter*, 89–90.

11. Hinrichs, *The Fateful Voyage of Captain Kidd*, 18.

12. *Abstracts of Wills on File in the Surrogate's Office, City of New York, 1665-1707*, 1:197; Library.cornell.edu/cgi/t/text/pageviewer-idx?c=nys; cc=nys;idno=nys054;q1=kidd;view=image;seq=220;size=75; page=root;print=1. Accessed March 2020.

13. Kenneth Scott and James A. Owre, *Genealogical Data from Data*

from Inventory of New York Estates 1666-1825 (New York: New York Genealogical and Biographical Society, 1970), 110.

14. *Abstracts of Wills on File in the Surrogate's Office, City of New York, 1665-1707*, 1:365.

15. http://www.bradleyfoundation.org/genealogies/Bingley/tobg04. htm#21952. Accessed March 28, 2020.

16. For a modern recipe of groaning cake see: https://www.pbs.org/ food/recipes/groaning-cake/#.Xfo51HNIGDU.email.

17. Hannah Woolley, *The Gentlewomans Companion or, A Guide to the Female Sex* (Devon, Great Britain: Prospect Books, 2001), 187.

18. John A. Grigg, *British Colonial America* (Santa Barbara, CA: ABC CLIO, 2008), 63.

19. Ibid.

20. Ibid., 65.

21. "New York Land Records, 1630-1975," images, *FamilySearch* (https://familysearch.org/ark:/61903/3:1:3QSQ-G9W5-GRHL? cc=2078654&wc=M7CX-B3X%3A358138101%2C360792501: 22 May 2014), New York > Conveyances 1683-1896 vol 18 > image 301 of 418; county courthouses, New York.

22. "New York Land Records, 1630-1975," images, *FamilySearch* (https://familysearch.org/ark:/61903/3:1:3QS7-99WG-K937- R?cc=2078654&wc=M7CX-BWP%3A358138101%2C360797701: 22 May 2014), New York > Conveyances 1698-1701 vol 23 > image 429 of 632; county courthouses, New York.

23. *Calendar of State Papers Colonial Series, America and West Indies*, no. 2459 and no. 2460, "Governor Fletcher to William Blathwayt," September 10, 1692.

24. Ibid.

6. The Golden Age of Piracy

1. Philip Gosse, *The History of Piracy* (New York: Dover Publications, 2007), 176.

2. Carl Bridenbaugh, *Fat Mutton and Liberty of Conscience: Society in Rhode Island, 1636-1690* (Providence: Brown University Press, 1974), 130.

3. Ibid., 188.

4. Hubert Jules Deschamps, *Les Pirates á Madagascar* (Paris: Berger-Levrault, 1972) quoted from Zacks, *The Pirate Hunter*, 41.

5. Marcus Rediker, *Villains of all Nations: Atlantic Pirates in the Golden Age* (Boston: Beacon Press, 2004), 87.

6. Ritchie, *Captain Kidd and the War Against the Pirates*, 59.

7. Rediker, *Villains of all Nations*, 93.

8. Alexander O. Exquemelin, translated by Alexis Brown. *The Buccaneers of America* (Harmondsworth, England: Penguin Books Ltd., 1969; Mineola, New York: Dover Publications, 2000), 10.

9. Joel H. Baer, *Pirates of the British Isles* (Gloucestershire: Tempus Publishing, 2005), 19.

10. David Cordingly, *Under the Black Flag* (New York: Random House, 1995), 192.

11. Robert C. Ritchie, "Samuel Burgess, Pirate," in *Authority and Resistance in Early New York*, eds. William Pencak and Conrad Edick Wright (New York: New York Historical Society, 1988), 131.

12. George Francis Dow and John Henry Edmonds, *The Pirates of the New England Coast 1630-1730* (New York: Dover Publications, 1996), 197.

13. David Cordingly, *Spanish Gold* (London: Bloomsbury, 2011), 255, cited in his footnote 27, HCA.1/99.3, PRO.

14. Joel Baer, ed., *British Piracy in the Golden Age: History and Interpretation, 1660-1730* (London: Pickering and Chatto, 2007), 1:340. This is a copy of the deposition of George Gibson from December 9, 1721, published in Philadelphia in the December 7-12, 1721, *American Weekly Mercury*.

15. Kenneth J. Kinkor, interview with author by telephone, McLean, Virginia, March 1, 2006.

16. Rediker, *Villains of all Nations*, 10.

17. Ritchie, "Samuel Burgess, Pirate," in *Authority and Resistance in Early New York*, 131.

18. Gosse, *The History of Piracy*, 321.

19. John C. Appleby, *Women and English Piracy 1540-1720* (Woodbridge, UK: The Boydell Press, 2013), 2.

20. C.R. Pennell, ed., *Bandits at Sea: A Pirates Reader* (New York: New York University Press, 2001), 198–199.

21. Marcus Rediker, *Between the Devil and the Deep Blue Sea*, "The Seaman as Pirate" (Cambridge: Cambridge University Press, 1987), 256.

22. Brett Rushfort and Paul W. Mapp, *Colonial North America and the Atlantic World: A History in Documents* (Upper Saddle River, New Jersey: Pearson Prentice Hall, 2009), 180.

23. "The term buccaneer is generally used now to describe the privateers and pirates of the West Indies who raided Spanish towns and shipping in the Caribbean and along the coasts of Central and South America in the period from around 1600 to the 1680s. The word originally applied to the groups of men, mainly French, who lived off the wild herds of cattle that roamed the northern regions

of Hispaniola. They became known as *boucaniers* or *bucaniers* from their practice of roasting meat on a *boucan*, a type of barbecue, in the manner of the local Indigenous people. Armed with an assortment of weapons and dressed in bloodstained hides, these rough men were described by a French missionary as the butcher's vilest servants who have been eight days in the slaughterhouse without washing themselves. Driven off Hispaniola by the Spanish in the 1630s, they migrated to the rocky island of Tortuga and used this as a base from which to attack passing ships and particularly those of the hated Spanish. After the capture of Jamaica by the British in 1655 many of the buccaneers moved to the harbor and town of Port Royal, which soon acquired the reputation of being the wickedest city in Christendom. The successive Governors of Jamaica encouraged the buccaneers to base themselves at Port Royal and issued privateering commissions for their ships. The buccaneers' presence protected the island from attack by the French or Spanish; and the ships and loot which they seized were of considerable benefit to the island's economy." David Cordingly, *Spanish Gold* (London; Bloomsbury, 2011), 8.

24. Exquemelin, *The Buccaneers of America*, 18.

25. Dow and Edmonds, *The Pirates of the New England Coast 1630-1730*, 228.

26. Exquemelin, *The Buccaneers of America*, 53–54; Joel H. Baer, "The Complicated Plot of Piracy: Aspects of English Criminal Law and the Image of the Pirate in Defoe," *The Eighteenth Century*, vol. 23, no. 1, (Winter 1982): 23.

27. Some historians, Robert C. Ritchie and Hans Turley, have suggested that pirates lived in a male-only homosexual world, but they bring forward little evidence in support of their assertions. I do not think the partnership of two pirates in the contract of matelotage was a partnership between two gay men.

28. Exquemelin, *The Buccaneers of America*, 53–54.

29. Kenneth J. Kinkor, interview with author by telephone, McLean, Virginia, March 1, 2006.

30. Malcolm Cowley, "The Sea Jacobins," *The New Republic*, February 1, 1933, 329.

31. Peter Earle, *The Pirate Wars* (New York: Thomas Dunne Books, 2003), 164.

32. Rediker, *Villains of all Nations*, 68.

33. David Cordingly, *Spanish Gold*, 18.

34. Exquemelin, *The Buccaneers of America*, 70.

35. Ibid., 71.

36. Ibid.

37. Ibid.

38. Ibid.

39. Ibid., 72.

40. Dow and Edmonds, *The Pirates of the New England Coast 1630-1730*, 163.

41. Joel Baer, ed., *British Piracy in the Golden Age: History and Interpretation, 1660-1730* (London: Pickering and Chatto, 2007), 2:xix.

42. Cordingly, *Under the Black Flag*, 229.

43. Baer, ed., *British Piracy in the Golden Age: History and Interpretation, 1660-1730*, 2:xii.

44. Joel Baer, ed., *British Piracy in the Golden Age*, 2:xii. Baer cited this quote in his text as from James F. Stephen. More information is in his footnote 19.

45. Cordingly, *Under the Black Flag*, 228.

7. Fletcher's Friends

1. *Calendar of State Papers Colonial Series, America and West Indies*, no. 473, "Governor the Earl of Bellomont to Council of Trade and Plantations," May 18, 1698.

2. Ibid.

3. *Calendar of State Papers Colonial Series, America and West Indies*, no. 1077, "Benjamin Fletcher to Council of Trade and Plantations," December 24, 1698.

4. *Calendar of State Papers Colonial Series, America and West Indies*, no. 473, "Governor the Earl of Bellomont to Council of Trade and Plantations," May 18, 1698.

5. Ibid.

6. *Calendar of State Papers Colonial Series, America and West Indies*, xxi, no. 2459 and no. 2460, "Governor Fletcher to William Blathwayt," September 10, 1692.

7. *Calendar of State Papers Colonial Series, America and West Indies*, no. 15, "Governor Fletcher to the Lords of Trade and Plantations," May 30, 1696; Burrows and Wallace, *Gotham: A History of New York City to 1898*, 106.

8. Ibid.

9. Burrows and Wallace, *Gotham: A History of New York City to 1898*, 105.

10. Earle, *Colonial Days in Old New York*, 156.

11. *Calendar of State Papers Colonial Series, America and West Indies*, no. 15, "Governor Fletcher to the Lords of Trade and Plantations," May 30, 1696; Burrows and Wallace, *Gotham: A History of New York City to 1898*, 106.

12. HCA 1/98 f. 85, PRO. Captain Samuel Burgess's Cargo list of the Margaret.

13. HCA 1/98 f. 42, PRO. "Deposition of Captain Samuel Burgess," March 1699.

14. Burrows and Wallace, *Gotham: A History of New York City*, 106–107.

15. Wilkins, *Captain Kidd and His Skeleton Island*, 30.

16. Earle, *Colonial Days in Old New York*, 102–103.

17. I.N. Phelps Stokes, *The Iconography of Manhattan Island 1498-1909*, (New York: Robert H. Dodd Publisher, 1915), 1:182.

18. Ibid.

19. Ibid., 184.

20. Ritchie, *Captain Kidd and the War Against the Pirates*, 27.

21. Burrows and Wallace, *Gotham: A History of New York City to 1898*, 112.

22. HCA 13-81-001, PRO, sworn statement of William Kidd dated October 15, 1695, giving his age and birthplace; Hinrichs, *The Fateful Voyage of Captain Kidd*, 17.

23. William J. Broad, "Seeking Pirate Treasure: Captain Kidd's Sunken Ship" in the *New York Times*, February 22, 2000.

8. London

1. Coughlin, *One Colonial Woman's World: The Life and Writings of Mehetabel Chandler Coit*, 27.

2. Robert T. Augustyn and Paul E. Cohen, *Manhattan in Maps 1527-1995* (New York: Rizzoli International Publications, 1997), 52.

3. Wilkins, *Captain Kidd and His Skeleton Island*, 193.

4. John Romeyn Brodhead, "Letter of Lord Bellomont to Secretary Vernon, October 10, 1700" in *Documents Relating to the Colonial History of New York* (Albany: Weed, Parsons and Company, 1853), 4:759–760.

5. Hinrichs, *The Fateful Voyage of Captain Kidd*, 28.

6. Ibid.

7. *Calendar of State Papers Colonial Series, America and West Indies*, no. 932, "Earl of Bellomont to William Popple," April 14, 1697.

8. Thomas Green, *The Tryal of Captain Thomas Green and his crew, pursued before the judge of the High Court of Admiralty of Scotland; And the Assessors appointed by the Lords of Privy Council*, 6 [book online](Edinburgh: printed by the heirs and successors of Andrew Anderson, Printer to the Queens most excellent Majesty, 1705); available from *Eighteenth Century Collections Online*, http://find.galegroup.com. proxy.library.georgetown.edu/ecco/infomark.do?type=search& tabID=T001&queryId=Locale%28en%2C%2C%29%3AFQE%3 D%28BN%2CNone%2C7%29N013613%24&sort=Author&search-Type=AdvancedSearchForm&version=1.0&userGroupName= wash43584&prodId=ECCO. Accessed February 8, 2013.

9. Cornelius Neale Dalton, *The Real Captain Kidd* (New York: Duffield and Co., 1911), 229–238.

10. Baer, *Pirates of the British Isles*, 93.

11. Ibid., 100.

12. Ibid., 101–102.

13. John Franklin Jameson, ed., C.O. 323:2, no. 124, I PRO, Footnote 1 in *Privateering and Piracy in the Colonial Period: Illustrative Documents* (Gloucester, United Kingdom: Dodo Press, 2008), 217.

14. Innes, *New Amsterdam and Its People*, 254.

15. Don C. Seitz, ed., *The Tryal of Capt. William Kidd: for Murther &
    Piracy* (New York: Rufus Rockwell Wilson, 1936), 7.

16. Ritchie, *Captain Kidd and the War Against the Pirates*, 54–55.

17. Baer, *Pirates of the British Isles*, 121.

18. Ibid.

19. Dalton, *The Real Captain Kidd*, 250–251.

20. Ibid., 238–250.

21. Kidd worked with Colonel Hewson in 1688 to fight off the French
    for Governor Codrington. Hewson testified in support of Kidd at
    his trial. He said Kidd told him this information about Bellomont
    and Livingston. This is found in Howell's *State Trials, Hewson's
    testimony*, 14:208.

22. Seitz, ed., *The Tryal of Capt. William Kidd: for Murther & Piracy*, 64.

23. Ibid., 64–66.

24. Ibid.

25. Portland MSS., Harley papers, vol. 25, f. 213; also, vol. 36, f. 72.

26. Hinrichs, *The Fateful Voyage of Captain Kidd*, 35.

27. New York Title and Guarantee Company, *New York Land-Holding
    Sea Rover* (New York: Lotus Press, 1901), 1–5.

9. Provisioning in New York

1. C.O. 323:2, no. 124 I, PRO, Footnote 1 in Jameson, ed., *Privateering and Piracy in the Colonial Period: Illustrative Documents*, 217.

2. Ritchie, *Captain Kidd and the War Against the Pirates*, 58.

3. Ibid.

4. HCA 1/15, PRO.

5. Wilkins, *Captain Kidd and His Skeleton Island*, 28.

6. William Berrian, *An Historical Sketch of Trinity Church, New York* (New York: Stanford and Swords, 1847), 24.

7. www.slaveryinnewyork.org/history.htm. Accessed March 26, 2020.

8. Clifford P. Morehouse, *Trinity: Mother of Churches* (New York: The Seabury Press, 1973), 18.

9. Ibid.

10. Sarah's Last Will and Testament had very strong religious overtones and strong biblical directives that she implored her adult children to follow after her death.

11. Author interview with Whitey Flynn, Assistant Archivist of Trinity Church, March 2020, by phone; I.N. Phelps Stokes, *The Iconography of Manhattan Island 1498-1909* (New York: Arno Press, 1967), 1:183.

12. The New York Genealogical and Biographical Society, "Records of Trinity Church Parish New York City," in *The New York Genealogical and Biographical Record*, vol. 67, no. 3, July 1936.

13. Earle, *Colonial Days in Old New York*, 275.

14. Ibid., 207–209.

15. Ritchie, *Captain Kidd and the War Against the Pirates*, 70.

16. Ibid., 64.

17. Burrows and Wallace, *Gotham: A History of New York City to 1898*, 113.

18. *The New York Genealogical and Biographical Record*, 140:106; "New York Land Records, 1630-1975," images, FamilySearch (https://familysearch.

org/ark:/61903/3:1:3QS7-99W5-G5X3?cc=2078654&wc=M7CX-B3X%3A358138101%2C360792501: 22 May 2014), New York > Conveyances 1683-1896 vol 18 > image 254,293,294 of 418; county courthouses, New York.

19. Ritchie, *Captain Kidd and the War Against the Pirates*, 66.

20. HCA 1/15, pt. 1, fol. 8, PRO. Kidd's contract is dated September 10, 1695.

21. Hinrichs, *The Fateful Voyage of Captain Kidd*, 34.

22. Pennybacker, "Captain Kidd: Hung, Not for Piracy but for Causing the Death of a Rebellious Seaman Hit with a Toy Bucket" in *New York History*, 485; Ritchie, *Captain Kidd and the War Against the Pirates*, 59.

23. Fletcher to the Board of Trade, July 1696, in New York Colonial Documents, 4:273-276, as cited by Ritchie, *Captain Kidd and the War Against the Pirates*, 68.

24. C.O. 5:860, no. 64 XXV, PRO, in Jameson, ed. *Privateering and Piracy in the Colonial Period: Illustrative Documents*, 239.

25. Ritchie, *Captain Kidd and the War Against the Pirates*, 61.

26. Ibid., 69.

10. Waiting

1. Lankevich, *New York City: A Short History*, 31.

2. Valentine, *History of the City of New York*, 215.

3. Ibid.

4. HCA 1/98 f. 116, PRO, Letter from Ede Wilday to her husband Richard Wilday, June 1698.

5. Jill Lepore, *New York Burning* (New York: Vintage Books, 2005), 235.

6. James Emott generously gave four pistoles, a Spanish coin sometimes called a doubloon, for the construction of the church.

7. Matson, *Merchants & Empire Trading in Colonial New York*, 63–64.

8. Bellomont's speech about pirates is in CO 5/1040, fols. 133–134, PRO.

9. HCA 1/98 fol. 209, PRO, Letter to Captain Kidd from James Emott, June 4, 1698, from New York.

10. HCA 1/98 fol. 128, second copy fol. 214 PRO Letter from Lord Bellomont to Captain Kidd written from New York, June 8, 1698.

11. HCA 1/98 f. 118, PRO, Letter from Sarah Horne to husband Jacob Horne, June 5, 1698.

11. Emott's Secret

1. Edwin Francis Hatfield, *History of Elizabeth, New Jersey: Including the Early History of Union County* (Carlisle, MA: Applewood Books, 1868), 257. Accessed September 1, 2018. https://books. google.com/books?id=qMrMmjsinxAC&pg=PA257&lpg=PA257& dq=james+emo tt+lawyer+in+ny+in+1699&source=bl&ots=_89_ zPXgUS&sig=metjq_WnO1JmYcG_wyxUC5 NNt9s&hl=en&sa =X&ved=2ahUKEwibz5P6hs_eAhUJvlMKHdQ0DdUQ6AEw-BXoECAQQA Q#v=onepage&q=james%20emott%20lawyer%20 in%20ny%20in%201699&f=false.

2. Ritchie, *Captain Kidd and the War Against the Pirates*, 173; Zacks, *The Pirate Hunter*, 226.

3. *Calendar of State Papers Colonial Series, America and West Indies*, no. 740 XVII, Copy of Minutes of Council of New York, July 20, 1699.

4. *Calendar of State Papers Colonial Series, America and West Indies*, no. 680 vi. "Letter to Lord Bellomont from Captain Kidd," June 24, 1699.

5. C.O. 323:2, no. 124 I, PRO, Footnote 1 in Jameson, ed., *Privateering and Piracy in the Colonial Period: Illustrative Documents*, 217.

6. Zacks, *The Pirate Hunter*, 226.

7. Petition of Sarah Kidd, July 16, 1699, Massachusetts State Archives, vol. 62, no. 316; Wilkins, *Captain Kidd and His Skeleton Island*, 141, "Statement by Duncan Campbell to Governor Bellomont." July 12, 1699, Boston. Campbell said Kidd gave him 90-100 pieces of eight (New York money) which he said was Sarah's money for charges and things Duncan Campbell bought for him.

8. Petition of Sarah Kidd, July 16, 1699, Massachusetts State Archives, vol. 62, no. 316.

9. Zacks, *The Pirate Hunter*, 240.

12. Taking Precautions

1. Massachusetts Historical Society Proceedings, 22:123–131, Jameson, ed. *Privateering and Piracy in the Colonial Period: Illustrative Documents*, 259; Dow and Edmonds, *The Pirates of the New England Coast 1630-1730*, 73.

2. C.O. 5:860, no. 62, PRO, "Lord Bellomont to the Board of Trade," July 8, 1699.

3. C.O. 5:860, no. 64, PRO, *Calendar of State Papers Colonial Series, America and West Indies*, no. 680, "Governor the Earl of Bellomont to the Council of Trade and Plantations," Boston, July 26, 1699.

4. Ibid.

5. Innes, *New Amsterdam and Its People*, 259.

6. Examination of Hugh Parrot, July 10, 1699, in Dalton, *The Real Captain Kidd*, 291.

7. *Calendar of State Papers Colonial Series, America and West Indies*,

no. 680, "Governor the Earl of Bellomont to the Council of Trade and Plantations," July 26, 1699.

8. C.O. 5:860, no. 62, PRO, Letter from the Earl of Bellomont to the Lords of Trade and Plantations, Boston, July 8, 1699, in Jameson, ed., *Privateering and Piracy in the Colonial Period: Illustrative Documents*, 243.

9. C.O. 5:860, no. 64 XXI, PRO, "Narrative of John Gardiner," July 17, 1699, in Jameson, ed., *Privateering and Piracy in the Colonial Period: Illustrative Documents*, 251.

10. Examination of William Jenkins, C.O. 5:860, fols. 174–176, PRO; Barleycorn, C.O. 5:860, fol. 176, PRO; C.O. 5:860, no. 64 XXI, PRO, "Narrative of John Gardiner," July 17, 1699, in Jameson, ed., *Privateering and Piracy in the Colonial Period: Illustrative Documents*, 251.

11. C.O. 5:860, no. 64 XXI, PRO, "Narrative of John Gardiner," July 17, 1699, in Jameson, ed., *Privateering and Piracy in the Colonial Period: Illustrative Documents*, 251.

12. C.O. 5:860, no. 64 XXI, PRO, Commons Journal, XIII, 30–31. "Narrative of John Gardiner," July 17, 1699, in Jameson, ed., *Privateering and Piracy in the Colonial Period: Illustrative Documents*, 253.

13. David Gardiner, "The Gardiner Family and the Lordship and Manor of Gardiner's Island," in the *New York Genealogical and Biographical Record*, vol. 23, no. 4, October 1892, 178.

14. C.O. 5:860, no. 64 XXI, PRO, "Narrative of John Gardiner." July 17, 1699.

13. Safe Haven on Block Island

1. *Calendar of State Papers Colonial, America and West Indies*, no. 680 xi, July 6, 1699.

2. Samuel Truesdale Livermore, *The History of Block Island: From its*

Discovery, in 1514 To the Present Time, 1876 (Hartford: The Case, Lockwood & Brainard Co., 1877), 268.

3. Colin Woodward, *The Republic of Pirates* (New York: Harcourt, 2007), 96.

4. *Calendar of State Papers Colonial Series, America and West Indies*, NO. 228, "Minutes of Council of Massachusetts," April 1, 1699; *Calendar of State Papers Colonial Series, America and West Indies*, no. 343, "Governor the Earl of Bellomont to Council of Trade and Plantations," May 3, 1699; Livermore, *The History of Block Island*, 115.

5. Ibid., 237.

6. Livermore, *The History of Block Island*, 188. In 1700 the population was 550 people—350 of them were Indigenous people. Kidd arrived in June 1699 so I have estimated the population to be approximately 550.

7. Ibid., 274.

8. Ibid., 268–286.

9. George R. Burgess and Jane Fletcher Fiske, *New Shoreham Town Record Book 1, from dates 1666-1717*, Manuscript transcription (Boston: The New England Historic Genealogical Society, 1924), 433.

14. Reunited

1. *Calendar of State Papers, Colonial Series, America and West Indies*, August 28, 1699, no. 746.

2. Wilkins, *Captain Kidd and His Skeleton Island*, 288.

3. C.O. 5:860, no.65 XIX, PRO, *Declaration of William Kidd*, September 4, 1699.

4. C.O. 5:860 no. 64 IV, PRO, Memorial of Duncan Campbell, June 19, 1699.

5.   Zacks, *The Pirate Hunter*, 120.

6.   C.O. 5:860, no. 64 XXV, PRO, Narrative of William Kidd, July 7, 1699.

7.   *Abstracts of Wills on File in the Surrogate's Office, City of New York 1665-1707*. http://www.blacksheepancestors.com/pirates/kidd.shtml. Accessed November 18, 2018.

8.   Ralph Paine, *The Book of Buried Treasure* (New York: The Macmillan Company, 1926), 62–63.

9.   C.O. 5:860, no. 64 XXV, PRO, Narrative of William Kidd, July 7, 1699.

10.   C.O. 5:860, no. 64 XXV, PRO, Narrative of William Kidd, July 7, 1699.

11.   "Information of Henry Bolton," February 4, 1701 in Jameson, ed., *Privateering and Piracy in the Colonial Period: Illustrative Documents*, 277-280.

12.   Ibid.

15. Accomplice

1.   C.O. 5:714, no. 70 VI, PRO, "Deposition of Theophilus Turner." Gilliam murdered Captain Edgecombe, commander of the *Mocha* frigate for the East India Company.

2.   *Calendar of State Papers, Colonial Series, America and West Indies*, no. 680 vi, "Captain Kidd to Lord Bellomont," June 24, 1699.

3.   Ibid.

4.   Ibid.

16. Buried Treasure

1.   C.O. 5:860, no. 64 XXI, PRO, *Commons Journal*, XIII, 30–31.

"Narrative of John Gardiner," July 17, 1699, in Jameson, ed., *Privateering and Piracy in the Colonial Period: Illustrative Documents*, 251–254.

2. All of Kidd's treasure was rumored to be "near half a million sterling in bullion" or about $88 million in today's dollars. *Calendar of State Papers Colonial America and West Indies*, no. 740 XIII.

3. *Calendar of State Papers Colonial, America and West Indies*, no. 746 XIX Boston, "Deposition of Captain Kidd," September 4, 1699.

4. *Calendar of State Papers Colonial, America and West Indies*, no. 746 XIX Boston, "Deposition of Captain Kidd," September 4, 1699; C.O. 5:860, no. 64 XXI, PRO, *Commons Journal*, XIII, 30–31; "Narrative of John Gardiner," July 17, 1699, in Jameson, ed., *Privateering and Piracy in the Colonial Period: Illustrative Documents*, 251–254.

5. C.O. 5:860, no. 64 XXI, PRO, *Commons Journal*, XIII, 30–31. "Narrative of John Gardiner," July 17, 1699, in Jameson, ed., *Privateering and Piracy in the Colonial Period: Illustrative Documents*, 251–254.

6. As reported by David Lion Gardiner, the sixteenth lord of the manor of Gardiner's Island, in a YouTube video of Gardiner's Island in 1978.

7. www.rdlgfoundation.org.

8. Wilkins, *Captain Kidd and His Skeleton Island*, 141. "Statement by Duncan Campbell to Governor Bellomont." July 12, 1699, Boston.

9. A 1978 YouTube video of David Gardiner, the sixteenth lord of the manor of Gardiner's Island, reported that his grandmother installed the marker where Kidd buried treasure and it was visible then.

10. Zacks, *The Pirate Hunter*, 242.

11. C.O. 5:860, no. 64 XXI, PRO, *Commons Journal*, XIII, 30–31. "Narrative of John Gardiner," July 17, 1699, in Jameson, ed., *Privateering and Piracy in the Colonial Period: Illustrative Documents*, 251–254.

12. Ibid., 253.

13. Ibid., 251.

14. Ibid., 252.

15. Wilkins, *Captain Kidd and His Skeleton Island*, 282.

16. Pennybacker, "Captain Kidd: Hung, Not for Piracy but for Causing the Death of a Rebellious Seaman Hit with a Toy Bucket" in *New York History*, 498.

17. *Calendar of State Papers Colonial, America and West Indies*, no. 1011 IX "Deposition of Mary Sands," August 7–10, 1699.

18. Wilkins, *Captain Kidd and His Skeleton Island*, 289.

19. Ibid.

20. William P. Quinn, *Shipwrecks around Cape Cod* (Orleans, MA: Lower Cape Publishing, 1973), 7.

21. Wilkins, *Captain Kidd and His Skeleton Island*, 289.

22. Ibid.

23. Ibid.

24. *Calendar of State Papers Colonial North America the West Indies*, no. 680 IX, "Examination of William Jenkins," July 6, 1699.

25. Some pirates, like Thomas Paine, went on to marry a governor's daughter. Henry Morgan became the lieutenant governor of Jamaica.

26. Zacks, *The Pirate Hunter*, 392.

17. Confronting Bellomont

1. Hinrichs, *The Fateful Voyage of Captain Kidd*, 178.

2. Wilkins, *Captain Kidd and His Skeleton Island*, 141.

3. Williard Hallam Bonner, "Clamors and False Stories the Reputa-

tion of Captain Kidd," *New England Quarterly* 17, no. 2 (June, 1944), 191; Ritchie, *Captain Kidd and the War Against the Pirates*, 180.

4. Pennybacker, "Captain Kidd: Hung, Not for Piracy but for Causing the Death of a Rebellious Seaman Hit with a Toy Bucket" in *New York History*, 498.

5. C.O. 5:860, no. 64, PRO, "Lord Bellomont to the Board of Trade," July 26, 1699, in Jameson, ed., *Privateering and Piracy in the Colonial Period: Illustrative Documents*, 258.

6. Justin Winsor, ed., *The Memorial History of Boston, Including Suffolk County, Massachusetts, 1630-1880*, vol. 2 (Boston: Ticknor and Company, 1881), 185.

7. Hinrichs, *The Fateful Voyage of Captain Kidd*, 131.

8. *Calendar of State Papers Colonial Series: America and West Indies*, no. 680 XXIV, "Examination of Captain Kidd before the Governor and Council," July 3, 1699,

9. Ritchie, *Captain Kidd and the War Against the Pirates*, 181.

10. Pennybacker, "Captain Kidd: Hung, Not for Piracy but for Causing the Death of a Rebellious Seaman Hit with a Toy Bucket" in *New York History*, 499.

11. *Calendar of State Papers Colonial Series: America and West Indies*, no. 680 XXIV, "Examination of Captain Kidd before the Governor and Council," July 3, 1699.

18. Kidd's Narrative

1. *Calendar of State Papers Colonial Series: America and West Indies*, no. 680, "Letter from Lord Bellomont to the Board of Trade," July 26, 1699.

2. Ritchie, *Captain Kidd and the War Against the Pirates*, 93.

3. C.O. 5:860, no. 64 XXV, PRO, *Narrative of William Kidd*. July 7, 1699.

19. Bellomont's Secret

1. C.O. 5:860, no. 62, PRO, "Lord Bellomont to the Board of Trade," July 8, 1699, in Jameson, ed., *Privateering and Piracy in the Colonial Period: Illustrative Documents*, 245.

2. *Calendar of State Papers Colonial Series: America and West Indies*, vol. 17: "Preface" 1699 and Addenda 1621-1698 (1908), VII-LIX. http://www.british-history.ac.uk/report.aspx?compid=71017. Accessed: January 23, 2020.

3. Wilkins, *Captain Kidd and His Skeleton Island*, 289.

4. C.O. 5:860, no. 64, PRO, Lord Bellomont to Board of Trade, July 26, 1699, in Jameson, ed., *Privateering and Piracy in the Colonial Period: Illustrative Documents*, 261.

20. Imprisoned

1. Annie Haven Thwing, *The Crooked & Narrow Streets of Boston 1630-1822* (Boston: Marshall Jones Company, 1920), 94.

2. Samuel Sewall, *Diary of Samuel Sewall 1674-1729*, vol. 1 in the *Collections of the Massachusetts Historical Society*, vol. 5 (Boston: Published by the Society, 1878), 503.

3. C.O. 5:860, no. 64, PRO, Lord Bellomont to Board of Trade, July 26, 1699, in Jameson, ed., *Privateering and Piracy in the Colonial Period: Illustrative Documents*, 261.

4. Ibid.

5. Ibid., 258.

6. C.O. 5:860, no. 64, PRO, Lord Bellomont to Board of Trade, July 26, 1699, in Jameson, ed., *Privateering and Piracy in the Colonial Period: Illustrative Documents*, 258.

7. Petition of Sarah Kidd to Lord Bellomont, Massachusetts State Archives, Boston, vol. 62, no. 316.

8. Wilkins, *Captain Kidd and His Skeleton Island*, 282.

21. The Pirate's Wife

1. Thwing, *The Crooked & Narrow Streets of Boston 1630-1822*, 94.

2. C.O. 5:861, no. 4 XVIII, PRO, "Sarah Kidd to Thomas Payne," July 18, 1699, in Jameson, ed., *Privateering and Piracy in the Colonial Period: Illustrative Documents*, 255.

3. Ibid.

4. *Calendar of State Papers Colonial: America and West Indies*, no. 1011 XVII, "Examination of Andrew Knott, Boston, November 13-14, 1699."

5. C.O. 5:861, no. 4, PRO, "Lord Bellomont to the Board of Trade," November 29, 1699, in Jameson, ed., *Privateering and Piracy in the Colonial Period: Illustrative Documents*, 269.

6. Ibid.

7. *Calendar of State Papers Colonial, America and West Indies*, no. 1011, "Governor the Earl of Bellomont to the Council of Trade and Plantations," November 29, 1699.

8. Wilkins, *Captain Kidd and His Skeleton Island*, 138; Zacks, *The Pirate Hunter*, 264.

9. Massachusetts State Archives, Boston, Massachusetts, vol. 62, no. 316.

10. Ibid.

11. Zacks, *The Pirate Hunter*, 275.

12. *Calendar of State Papers Colonial: America and West Indies*, no. 952, "Lord Bellomont to the Lords of Trade," November 28, 1700.

13. Ibid.; Fernow Berthold, *New York (Colony) Council Calendar of Council Minutes 1668-1783* (Harrison, NY: Harbor Hills Books, 1987), 142.

14. Ibid., 138.

15. C.O. 5:860, no. 64 XXI, PRO, "Narrative of John Gardiner," July 17, 1699, in Jameson, ed., *Privateering and Piracy in the Colonial Period: Illustrative Documents*, 253.

16. Ibid., Footnote 6, 254.

17. Massachusetts State Archives, Boston, vol. 61, no. 317, July 25, 1699.

18. Petition of Sarah Kidd. July 25, 1699. Massachusetts State Archives, vol. 62, no. 317.

19. John Russell Bartlett, ed., *Records of the Colony of Rhode Island, vol. 3, 1678-1706* (Providence: A.C. Greene and Brothers, 1856), 393.

20. *Calendar of State Papers Colonial: America and West Indies*, no. 1011, "Governor the Earl of Bellomont to the Council of Trade and Plantations," November 29, 1699.

21. *Calendar of State Papers Colonial: America and West Indies*, no. 890, "Governor the Earl of Bellomont to the Council of Trade and Plantations," October 24, 1699.

22. Ibid.

23. *Calendar of State Papers Colonial: America and West Indies*, no. 1011, "Governor the Earl of Bellomont to the Council of Trade and Plantations," November 29, 1699.

24. *Calendar of State Papers Colonial: America and West Indies*, no. 929, "Governor the Earl of Bellomont to Mr. Popple," October 1699.

25. Walter A. Nebiker and David Chase, *Historic and Architectural Resources of Jamestown, Rhode Island* (Providence: Rhode Island Historical Preservation & Heritage Commission, 1995), 56–57.

26. *Calendar of State Papers Colonial: America and West Indies*, no. 668, "Minutes of the Council of New York."

27. C.O. 5:860, no. 64, PRO, "Lord Bellomont to the Board of Trade,"

July 26, 1699, in Jameson, ed., *Privateering and Piracy in the Colonial Period: Illustrative Documents*, 259.

28. Ibid., 260.

29. Ibid.

30. Mark Peterson, *The City-State of Boston* (Princeton: Princeton University Press, 2019), 199.

31. Winsor, ed., *The Memorial History of Boston, Including Suffolk County, Massachusetts, 1630-1880*, 179.

32. Charles E. Clark, *The Public Prints: The Newspaper in Anglo-American Culture, 1665-1740* (New York: Oxford University Press, 1994), 77.

33. Wilkins, *Captain Kidd and His Skeleton Island*, 140.

34. Zacks, *The Pirate Hunter*, 275.

35. Ibid.

36. *Calendar of State Papers Colonial Series: America and West Indies*, no. 14, Boston, "Lord Bellomont to the Lords of Trade, "January 5, 1700; Winsor, ed., *The Memorial History of Boston, Including Suffolk County, Massachusetts, 1630-1880*, 179.

37. *Calendar of State Papers Colonial Series: America and West Indies*, no. 14, Boston, "Lord Bellomont to the Lords of Trade," January 5, 1700.

38. C.O. 5:860, no. 64, PRO, Bellomont to Board of Trade, July 26, 1699, in Jameson, ed., *Privateering and Piracy in the Colonial Period: Illustrative Documents*, 261.

39. *Calendar of State Papers Colonial Series: America and West Indies*, no. 14, Boston, "Lord Bellomont to the Lords of Trade," January 5, 1700.

40. Captain William Kidd: https://www.ancestrylibrary.com/family-tree/person/tree/15990650; Sarah Bradley: https://www.ancestry

library.com/family-tree/person/tree/10138974/. Accessed March 1, 2018.

41. *Calendar of State Papers Colonial Series: America and West Indies*, no. 850, October 11, 1699.

42. Jameson, ed., *Privateering and Piracy in the Colonial Period: Illustrative Documents*, 217.

43. *Calendar of State Papers Colonial Series: America and West Indies*, no. 312, Whitehall, "Council of Trade and Plantations to Governor the Earl of Bellomont," April 11, 1700.

44. *Calendar of State Papers Colonial Series: America and West Indies*, no. 1015, November 30, 1699, Boston; Winsor, ed., *The Memorial History of Boston, Including Suffolk County, Massachusetts, 1630-1880*, 182.

45. *Calendar of State Papers Colonial Series*, no. 769, Boston, "Lord Bellomont to the Lords of the Admiralty," September 7, 1699.

46. *Calendar of State Papers Colonial Series*, no. 1015, November 30, 1699.

47. *Calendar of State Papers Colonial Series*, no. 746, "Governor the Earl of Bellomont to the Council of Trade," August 28, 1699.

48. Samuel Sewell, *Diary of Samuel Sewell, 1674-1729*, vol. 2, February 6, 1700, in https://babel.hathitrust.org/cgi/pt?id=hvd.hc4w42&view=1up&seq=152&q1=kidd. Accessed December 16, 2020.

22. The King's Ship

1. *Calendar of State Papers Colonial Series: America and West Indies*, no. 22, January 9, 1700.

2. *Calendar of State Papers Colonial Series: America and West Indies*, no. 890, "Governor the Earl of Bellomont to the Council of Trade and Plantations," October 24, 1699.

3. Zacks, *The Pirate Hunter*, 282.

4. Ibid., 277.

5. *Calendar of State Papers Colonial Series: America and West Indies*, no. 310, "Admiralty Office, List of Pirates," April 11, 1700.

6. Hinrichs, *The Fateful Voyage of Captain Kidd*, 135.

7. C.O. 5:787, fol. 289, PRO.

8. *Calendar of State Papers Colonial Series: America and West Indies*, no. 680, "Lord Bellomont to the Board of Trade," July 26, 1699.

9. Zacks, *The Pirate Hunter*, 277.

10. Ibid., 286.

11. Margarette Lincoln, *British Pirates and Society 1680-1730* (Burlington, VT: Ashgate Publishing Co., 2014), 199.

12. Zacks, *The Pirate Hunter*, 286.

13. Ibid.

14. Ibid.

15. Ibid.

23. Newgate

1. Hinrichs, *The Fateful Voyage of Captain Kidd*, 135.

2. Wilkins, *Captain Kidd and His Skeleton Island*, 184.

3. Ibid.

24. Kidd's Good Deed

1. HCA 24/127, April 1701, PRO. Petition of Elizabeth Mead, wife of Henry Mead and Gertrude Beck, wife of William Beck.

2. Zacks, *The Pirate Hunter*, 340.

3. HCA 24/127, April 1701, PRO. Petition of Elizabeth Mead, wife of Henry Mead and Gertrude Beck, wife of William Beck.

25. Trial

1. Earle, *Colonial Days in Old New York*, 307.

2. Valentine, *A History of the City of New York*, 210.

3. *Calendar of State Papers Colonial, America and West Indies*, no. 280, March 24, 1701.

4. *Calendar of State Papers Colonial: America and West Indies*, no. 769, "Countess Bellomont to Secretary Vernon," August 21, 1701.

5. William Kidd to the Speaker of the House of Commons (Robert Harley) in Jameson, ed., *Privateering and Piracy in the Colonial Period: Illustrative Documents*, 282.

6. www.oldbaileyonline.org/static/The-old-bailey.jsp#location. Accessed February 2, 2022.

7. John Riggs to Robert Livingston, Collection Reference Number GLC03107, The Livingston Family Papers [025]1699; John Nanfan to Robert Livingston, Collection Reference Number GLC03107.00599, The Livingston Family Papers [026] January-June 1700; James Graham to Robert Livingston Collection Reference Number GLC03107.00593 and GLC03107.00551, The Livingston Family Papers [026] January-June 1700; Duncan Campbell to Robert Livingston, The Livingston Family Papers, March 7, 1700.

8. James Graham to Robert Livingston, Collection Reference Number GLC03107.00551, The Livingston Family Papers [026] January–June 1700.

9. John Nanfan to Robert Livingston regarding a Parliamentary hearing on Captain William Kidd's Commission, Collection Reference Number GLC03107.00599, The Livingston Family Papers [026] January–June 1700.

10. *Calendar of State Papers Colonial: America and West Indies*, no. 205, March 4, 1701.

11. HCA 1/29, pt. 3, fol. 285, PRO.

12. Captain Charles Johnson, *A General History of the Pyrates*, edited by Manual Schonhorn (London: J.M. Dent & Sons, 1972; New York: Dover Publication, 1999), 450.

13. Baer, *Pirates of the British Isles*, 157.

14. Seitz, ed., *The Tryal of Capt. William Kidd: for Murther & Piracy*, 225–226.

15. Baer, *Pirates of the British Isles*, 159.

16. Hinrichs, *The Fateful Voyage of Captain Kidd*, 139.

26. Tragic News

1. E.B. O'Callaghan, ed. "Attorney-General Broughton to the Lord of Trade, September 3, 1701" in *Documents Relative to the Colonial History of the State of New York*, vol. 4 (Albany: Weed, Parsons, and Co., 1854), 914.

2. Seitz, ed., *The Tryal of Capt. William Kidd: for Murther & Piracy*, 227–30.

3. Edmund Baily O'Callaghan, *Lists of Inhabitants of Colonial New York Excerpted from The Documentary History of the State of New-York* (Baltimore: Genealogical Publishing Co., Inc., 1979), 23; Lepore, *New York Burning*, 235. Table 1 lists the population in 1703 as 4375.

4. Will of Samuel Bradley in *Abstracts of Wills on File in the Surrogate's Office, City of New York, 1665-1801*. 1:366–367.

5. Ibid.

6. Tuttle, *Abstracts of Farm Titles in the City of New York*, East Side, Between 75th and 120th Streets, 5.

7. *Calendar of State Papers Colonial: West Indies and America*, no. 1011,

Bellomont passed the information on to the Council of Trade and Plantations, November 29, 1699.

8. http://www.nytimes.com/2000/-2/22 science/seeking-pirate-treasure-captain-kidd-s-sunken-ship.html. "Seeking Pirate Treasure: Captain Kidd's Sunken Ship," by William J. Broad, February 22, 2000.

9. Goodfriend, *Before the Melting Pot: Society and Culture in Colonial New York City, 1664–1730*, 246, footnote 39.

27. New Beginnings

1. Tuttle, *Abstracts of Farm Titles in the City of New York*, East Side, Between 75th and 120th Streets, 4.

2. Ibid., 7

3. Christopher Rousby, https/www.ancestrylibrary.com/family-tree/person/tree/15990650. Accessed June 26, 2019.

4. Gideon J. Tucker, *Names of Persons for Whom Marriage Licenses Were Issued by the Secretary of the Province of New York Previous to 1784* (Albany: Weed, Parsons and Company, 1860), 189.

5. Tuttle, *Abstracts of Farm Titles in the City of New York, East Side, Between 75th and 120th Streets*, 7; Samuel Bradley to Christopher Rousby in New York Deeds, 1659–1846, 10:1–4.

6. E.B. O'Callaghan, *Calendar of New York Colonial Manuscripts Endorsed Land Papers in the Office of the Secretary of State of New York 1643-1803* (New York: Harbor Hill Books, 1987), 70.

7. Burrows and Wallace, *Gotham: A History of New York City to 1898*, 115.

8. Valentine, *History of the City of New York*, 253.

9. Tuttle, *Abstracts of Farm Titles in the City of New York, East Side, Between 75th and 120th Streets*, 7–8.

10. Ibid., 8.

11. Ibid.

12. Innes, *New Amsterdam and Its People*, 266.

13. Evelyn Sidman Wachter, *Sidman-Sidman Families of Upstate New York* (Baltimore: Gateway Press, Inc., 1981), 49.

14. Ibid.

15. https://babel.hathitrust.org/cgi/pt?id=hvd.32044097878532; view=2up;seq=318;size=125. Accessed March 15, 2021.

16. Wilkins, *Captain Kidd and His Skeleton Island, 272; Collections of the New York Historical Society for the Year 1885* (New York: New York Historical Society, 1885), 92.

17. Burrows and Wallace, *Gotham: A History of New York City to 1898*, 140.

18. Lincoln, *British Pirates and Society, 1680-1730*, 201.

19. C.O. 323:6, no. 79-81, PRO, also *Calendar of State Papers, Colonial: North America and the West Indies*, 620ii, vol. 24 (1709).

20. https://search.ancestrylibrary.com/cgi-bin/sse.dll?indiv=1&db=DictNatBiogV1&h=2939.

21. In 1932 the American scholar John Robert Moore announced at a literary meeting that after years of careful research he believed Captain Charles Johnson was the anonymous pen name for the novelist, journalist, and sometimes historian, Daniel Defoe. Professor Moore's reputation as the leading Defoe scholar convinced libraries around the world to recatalog *A General History of the Pyrates* with the author's name as Daniel Defoe. But in 1988 two scholars, P.N. Furbank and W.R. Owens, disputed the plausibility of Defoe as the author in their book *The Canonisation of Daniel Defoe*. Many scholars today accept the conclusion that Defoe could not have

penned the book, but there are those who also believe otherwise. The editor of the 1999 edition of *A General History of the Pyrates*, Manuel Schonhorn, believed Defoe was the author and dedicated the first five pages of the introduction to Defoe's life, works, and maritime interests. Although the identity of the author is unclear, it is certain that the book has greatly influenced the popular opinion of pirates from the eighteenth century to now. David Cordingly, *Under the Black Flag*, xx.

22. Johnson, *A General History of the Pyrates*, 6.

23. Ibid., 41.

24. Ibid., xxxiii.

25. Ibid.

26. *Boston News-Letter*, from Monday, June 26, to Monday, July 3, 1704, no. 11, Boston, Massachusetts.

27. Baer, ed., *British Piracy in the Golden Age*, 1:xxxiv.

28. Ibid., 13.

29. Ibid., xxxiv.

30. Ibid., 303. "The British Journal," no. 1, Saturday, September 22, 1722.

31. Ibid., xix.

32. Johnson, *A General History of the Pyrates*, xxxvi.

33. Wachter, *Sidman-Sidman Families of Upstate New York*, 52.

34. Will of Christopher Rousby in *Abstracts of Wills*, vol. 1, 1670-1730. *Archives of the State of New Jersey-First Series*, vol. 23, 395.

35. Ibid.

36. Ibid.

37. William Nelson, *Documents Relating to the Colonial History of the State of New Jersey*, vol. 13, *Calendar of New Jersey Wills*, vol. 1, 1670-1730 (Bowie, MD: Heritage Books, 1994), 395.

38. Dorothy Denneen Volo and James M. Volo, *Daily Life in the Age of Sail* (Westport: Greenwood Press, 2002), 5.

39. Nelson, *Documents Relating to the Colonial History of the State of New Jersey*, 395.

28. Full Circle

1. Augustyn and Cohen, *Manhattan in Maps 1527-1995*, 56; Good-friend, *Before the Melting Pot: Society and Culture in Colonial New York*, 113.

2. Augustyn and Cohen, *Manhattan in Maps 1527-1995*, 54. The map of Manhattan from 1730 was drawn by the cartographer James Lyne.

3. Goodfriend, *Before the Melting Pot: Society and Culture in Colonial New York*, 205–206.

4. Augustyn and Cohen, *Manhattan in Maps 1527-1995*, 54.

5. Will of Joseph Latham in *Abstracts of Wills on file in the Surrogate's office, City of New York, 1730-1744*, vol. 3, liber 11, 60–61.

6. Will of Sarah Rousby, *New York County, Wills and Administrations 1742-1751*, 15:262-264.

7. https://www.ancestryheritagequest.com/interactive/20637/dvm_LocHist006746-00166-1. James Riker, "The Annals of Newtown in Queens County, New-York: containing its history from its first settlement, together with many interesting facts concerning the adjacent towns: also, a particular account of numerous Long Island families now spread over this and various other states of the Union" (New York: D. Fanshaw, 1852), 303. Accessed February 3, 2021.

8. Will of Sarah Rousby, *New York County, Wills and Administrations 1742-1751*, 15:262–264.

9. Ibid.

10. Ibid.

11. Ibid.

12. Ibid.

13. Zimmerman, *The Women of the House*, 220.

14. Will of Sarah Rousby, *New York County, Wills and Administrations 1742-1751*, 15:262–264.

15. James Davey, ed., *Tudor & Stuart Seafarers: The Emergence of a Maritime Nation, 1485-1707* (London: Adlard Coles Bloomsbury Publishing, 2018), 237.

16. Nancy L. Struna, *People of Prowess: Sport, Leisure, and Labor in Early Anglo-America* (Chicago: University of Illinois Press, 1996), 146–147.

17. Struzinski, "The Tavern in Colonial America," 31; Struna, *People of Prowess: Sport, Leisure, and Labor in Early Anglo-America*, 147.

18. *The New-York Weekly Journal*, October 15, 1739. https://infoweb.newsbank.com/apps/readex/openurl?ctx_ver=z39.88-2004&rft_id=info%3Asid%2Finfoweb.newsbank.com&svc_dat=EANX&req_dat=0D52805756D8EA80&rft_val_format=info%3Aofi%2Ffmt%3Akev%3Amtx%3Actx&rft_dat=document_id%3Aimage%252Fv2%253A1036CD36DBC06A78%2540EANX-1062A47A62C49A1F%25402356504-1062A47AA84571FD%25403-1062A47AEF637380%2540. Accessed June 2019.

19. Lepore, *New York Burning*, 5.

20. Zimmerman, *The Women of the House*, 257.

21. Ibid.

22. Lepore, *New York Burning*, 45.

23. Ibid., 62.

24. Stokes, *The Iconography of Manhattan Island*, 196; Lankevich, *New York City: A Short History*, 37.

25. Burrows and Wallace, *Gotham: A History of New York City to 1898*, 160.

26. Ibid., 161.

27. Valentine, *History of the City of New York*, 268–276.

28. Lepore, *New York Burning*, 9.

29. Valentine, *History of the City of New York*, 268–276.

30. Ibid.

31. Lepore, *New York Burning*, 268, Appendix C.

32. Ibid.

33. Ibid., 105.

34. Ibid.

35. Lankevich, *New York City: A Short History*, 37.

36. Thomas L. Purvis, *Almanacs of American Life, Colonial America to 1763* (New York: Facts on File, Inc., 1999), 174.

37. Ibid., 173.

38. Will of Sarah Rousby, *New York County, Wills and Administrations 1742-1751*, 15:262–264.

39. Ibid.

40. Purvis, *Almanacs of American Life, Colonial America to 1763*, 174.

41. New York death record liber 15, 330.

42. Author interview with Kimberley Sulik, archivist/records manager, New York County Surrogate's Court, April 17, 2019, by email. Author interview with Rhonda McClure, genealogist with American Ancestors, in person, August 3, 2019, Boston, MA.

Bibliography

Augustyn, Robert T. and Paul E. Cohen. *Manhattan in Maps 1527-1995*. New York: Rizzoli International Publications, 1997.

Austin, John Osborne. *The Genealogical Dictionary of Rhode Island Comprising Three Generations of Settlers Who Came Before 1690*. Baltimore: Genealogical Publishing Company, 1969.

Austin Baxter Keep, Charles Alexander Nelson and Herbert L. Osgood. *Minutes of the Common Council of the City of New York 1675-1776*. New York: Dodd, Mead, 1905.

Baer, Joel. *Pirates of the British Isles*. Stroud, Gloucestershire: Tempus, 2005.

—. *British Piracy in the Golden Age: History and Interpretation, 1660-1730*. London: Pickering and Chatto, 2007.

Barrow, Ian. *The East India Company 1600-1858*. Indianapolis: Hackett Publishing Co., 2017.

Bartlett, John Russell. *Records of the Colony of Rhode Island and Providence Plantations in New England, vol. 3, 1678-1706*. Providence: A.C. Greene and Brothers, 1856.

Berkin, Carol. *First Generations, Women in Colonial America*. New York: Hill and Wang, 1996.

Berkin, Carol and Leslie Horowitz. *Women's Voices, Women's Lives: Documents in Early American History*. Boston: Northeastern University Press, 1998.

Bridenbaugh, Carl. *Cities in the Wilderness: The First Century of Urban Life in America 1625-1742*. New York: Capricorn Books, 1964.

Brodhead, John Romeyn. *Documents Relating to the Colonial History of the State of New-York*, vol. 3. Albany: Weed, Parsons and Company, 1853.

Burgess, George R. and Jane Fletcher Fiske. *New Shoreham Town Record Book 1, from dates 1666-1717*. Manuscript transcription, Boston: The New England Historic Genealogical Society, 1924.

Burrows, Edwin G. and Mike Wallace. *Gotham: A History of New York City to 1898*. New York: Oxford University Press, 1999.

Cabell, Craig, Graham A. Thomas and Allan Richards. *Captain Kidd: The Hunt for the Truth*. South Yorkshire: Pen & Sword Maritime, 2010.

Cawthorne, Nigel. *A History of Pirates: Blood and Thunder on the High Seas*. London: Arcturus Publishing Limited, 2011.

Christoph, Peter R. *The Leisler Papers, 1689-1691: Files of the Provincial Secretary of New York Relating to the Administration of Lieutenant-Governor Jacob Leisler*. New York: Syracuse University Press, 2002.

Christoph, Peter R. and Florence A., eds. *New York Historical Manuscripts: English Books of General Entries of the Colony of New York, 1674-1688*. Baltimore: Genealogical Publishing Co., 1982.

Clark, Charles E. *The Public Prints: The Newspaper in Anglo-American Culture, 1665-1740*. New York: Oxford University Press, 1994.

Coughlin, Michelle Marchetti. *One Colonial Woman's World: The Life and Writings of Mehetabel Chandler Coit.* Boston: University of Massachusetts Press, 2012.

Cox, Henry Miller. *The Cox Family in America: A History and Genealogy of the Older Branches of the Family from the Appearance of Its First Representative in this Country in 1610.* Somerville, New Jersey: The Unionist-Gazette Association, 1912.

Dalton, Cornelius Neale. *The Real Captain Kidd.* New York: Duffield and Co., 1911.

Davey, James, ed. *Tudor & Stuart Seafarers: The Emergence of a Maritime Nation, 1485-1707.* London: Adlard Coles Bloomsbury Publishing Plc., 2018.

De Peyster, Frederick. "The Life and Administration of Richard, Earl of Bellomont," an address delivered before the New York Historical Society, November 18, 1879. New York: *New York Historical Society Collections,* 1879.

Donnelly, Mark P. and Daniel Diehl. *Pirates of New Jersey.* Mechanicsburg, PA: Stackpole Books, 2010.

Dorman, Margaret Scoville. "Legend and Literature of Captain William Kidd" in *Connecticut Magazine* 1 (1905):269–279.

Dow, George Francis and John Henry Edmonds. *The Pirates of the New England Coast 1630-1730.* New York: Dover Publications, Inc., 1996.

Druett, Joan. *She Captains: Heroines and Hellions of the Sea.* New York: Barnes and Noble Books, 2000.

Duffy, John. *A History of Public Health in New York City 1625-1866.* New York: Russell Sage Foundation, 1968.

Earle, Alice Morse. *Colonial Days in Old New York.* Detroit: Singing Tree Press, 1968.

—. *Child Life in Colonial Times*. Mineola, New York: Dover Publications, 2009.

—. *Home Life in Colonial Days*. Middle Village, New York: Jonathan David Publishers, 1975.

Earle, Peter. *The Pirate Wars*. New York: Thomas Dunne Books, 2003.

Fernow, Berthold, and Arnold J. F. Van Laer. *Calendar of Council Minutes 1688-1783*. Harrison, NY: Harbor Bill Books, 1987.

Fernow, Berthold. *Calendar of Wills on File and Recorded in the Offices of the Clerk of the Court of Appeals, of the County Clerk at Albany, and of the Secretary of State. 1626-1836*. Baltimore: Genealogical Publishing Co., 1967.

Foote, Thelma Wills. *Black and White Manhattan: The History of Racial Formation in Colonial New York*. New York: Oxford University Press, 2004.

Goodfriend, Joyce. *Before the Melting Pot: Society and Culture in Colonial New York*. Princeton: Princeton University Press, 1994.

Grigg, John A., ed. *British Colonial America: People and Perspectives*. Santa Barbara, California: ABC-CLIO, 2008.

Hanna, Mark G. *Pirate Nests and the Rise of the British Empire, 1570-1740*. Chapel Hill: University of North Carolina Press, 2015.

Harris, Graham. *Treasure and Intrigue: The Legacy of Captain Kidd*. Toronto: A Hounslow Book, 2002.

Hastings, Hugh. *Documents of the Senate of the State of New York*, vol. 6, no. 11, pt. 3. Albany: Oliver A. Quayle State Legislative Printer, 1904.

Hinrichs, Dunbar Maury. *The Fateful Voyage of Captain Kidd*. New York: Bookman Associates, Inc., 1955.

—. *Mrs. Captain Kidd*. New York: Vantage Press Inc., 1952.

Innes, J.H. *New Amsterdam and Its People*. New York: Charles Scribner's Sons, 1902.

Jameson, John Franklin, ed. *Privateering and Piracy in the Colonial Period: Illustrative Documents*. Gloucester, United Kingdom: Dodo Press, 2008.

Knight, Sarah Kemble. *The Journal of Madam Knight*. Bedford, Massachusetts: Applewood Books, 1825.

Konstam, Angus. *The World Atlas of Pirates*. Guilford, Connecticut: The Lyons Press, 2010.

Kouwenhoven, John A. *The Columbia Historical Portrait of New York*. New York: Doubleday & Company, 1953.

Lankevich, George J. *New York City: A Short History*. New York: New York University Press, 2002.

Lepore, Jill. *New York Burning*. New York: Vintage Books, 2005.

Lincoln, Charles Z., William H. Johnson and A. Judd Northrup. *Colonial Laws of New York Year 1664 to the Revolution*, vol. 1. Albany: James B. Lyon, State Printer, 1894.

Lincoln, Margarette. *British Pirates and Society, 1680-1730*. Burlington: Ashgate Publishing Co., 2014.

—. *Naval Wives & Mistresses*. Gloucestershire: The History Press, 2011.

Livermore, Samuel Truesdale. *A History of Block Island: From its Discovery, in 1514, to the Present Time, 1876*. Hartford: The Case, Lockwood & Brainard Co., 1877.

Lockridge, Kenneth A. *Literacy in Colonial New England*. New York: W.W. Norton & Company, 1974.

Matson, Cathy. *Merchants & Empire Trading in Colonial New York*. Baltimore: The Johns Hopkins University Press, 1998.

Middleton, Simon. *From Privileges to Rights, Work and Politics in Colonial New York City*. Philadelphia: University of Pennsylvania Press, 2006.

Morehouse, Clifford P. *Trinity: Mother of Churches: An Informal History of Trinity Parish in the City of New York*. New York: Seabury Press, 1973.

Nebiker, Walter A. and David Chase. *Historic and Architectural Resources of Jamestown, Rhode Island*. Providence: Rhode Island Historical Preservation & Heritage Commission, 1995.

Nelson, William, ed. *Documents Relating to the Colonial History of the State of New Jersey, vol. 23, Calendar of New Jersey Wills*, vol. 1 1670-1730. Peterson, NJ: The Press Printing and Publishing Col, 1901.

New York State Secretary's Office. *Calendar of New York Colonial Manuscripts Indorsed Land Papers, 1643-1803*. Albany: Weed, Parsons & Co. Printers and Publishers, 1864.

O'Callaghan, Edmund Baily. *Lists of Inhabitants of Colonial New York Excerpted from The Documentary History of the State of New-York*. Baltimore: Genealogical Publishing Co., Inc. 1979.

—. *Calendar of New York Colonial Manuscripts Indorsed Land Papers in the Office of the Secretary of State of New York 1643-1803*. New York: Harbor Hill Books, 1987.

O'Callaghan, E.B., ed. *Documents Relative to the Colonial History of the State of New York*, vols. 3, 4. Albany: Weed, Parsons, and Co., 1854.

Paine, Ralph D. *The Book of Buried Treasure*. New York: The Macmillan Company, 1926.

Palfrey, John Gorham. *History of New England*, vol. 4. Boston: Little, Brown, and Company, 1875.

Parker, Lucretia. *Piratical Barbarity, Or, The Female Captive: Comprising the Particulars of the Capture of the English Sloop Eliza-Ann, On Her Passage from St. Johns to Antigua, the Horrid Massacre of the Unfortunate Crew by the*

Pirates, March 12, 1825: And the Unparalled Sufferings of Miss Lucretia Parker. Providence: Printed for Wm. Avery, 1825.

Pennell, C.R., ed. *Bandits at Sea: A Pirates Reader.* New York: New York University Press, 2001.

Purvis, Thomas L. *Colonial America to 1763.* New York: Facts on File, Inc., 1999.

Rediker, Marcus. *Between the Devil and the Deep Blue Sea: Merchant Seamen, Pirates and the Anglo-American Maritime World, 1700-1750.* New York: Cambridge University Press, 1987.

—. *Villains of All Nations: Atlantic Pirates in the Golden Age.* Boston: Beacon Press, 2004.

Ritchie, Robert C. *Captain Kidd and the War Against the Pirates.* Cambridge: Harvard University Press, 1986.

Rogozinski, Jan. *Honor Among Thieves.* Mechanicsburg, PA: Stackpole Books, 2000.

Seitz, Don C. *The Tryal of Capt. William Kidd: for Murther & Piracy.* New York: Rufus Rockwell Wilson, 1936.

Sheffield, William P. *A Historical Sketch of Block Island.* Newport: John P. Sanborn & Co, Mercury Office Printers, 1876.

Shorto, Russell. *The Island at the Center of the World.* New York: Vintage Books, 2004.

Singleton, Esther. *Social New York Under the Georges 1714-1776.* New York: D. Appleton and Co., 1902.

Stokes, I.N. Phelps. *The Iconography of Manhattan Island, 1498-1909,* vol. 1. New York: Robert H. Dodd Publisher, 1915.

Struna, Nancy L. *People of Prowess Sport, Leisure, and Labor in Early Anglo-America.* Chicago: University of Illinois Press, 1996.

Struzinski, Steven. "The Tavern in Colonial America," *The Gettysburg Historical Journal* 1, Article 7, 2002.

Thwing, Annie Haven. *The Crooked & Narrow Streets of Boston 1630-1822.* Boston: Marshall Jones Company, 1920.

Tucker, Gideon J. *Names of Persons for Whom Marriage Licenses Were Issued by the Secretary of the Province of New York Previous to 1784.* Albany: Weed, Parsons and Company, 1860.

Valentine, David T. *History of the City of New York.* New York: G.P. Putnam & Co., 1853.

Van Laer, A.J.F., ed. *Correspondence of Maria van Rensselaer.* Albany: The University of the State of New York, 1935.

Wilkins, Harold T. *Captain Kidd and His Skeleton Island.* New York: Liveright Publishing Corporation, 1937.

Wilson, Rufus Rockwell. *Historic Long Island.* New York: The Berkeley Press, 1902.

Winsor, Justin, ed. *The Memorial History of Boston including Suffolk County, Massachusetts. 1630-1880,* vol. 2. Boston: James R. Osgood and Company, 1881.

Winston, Alexander. *No Man Knows My Grave: Privateers and Pirates 1665-1715.* Boston: Houghton Mifflin, 1969.

Woodward, Colin. *The Republic of Pirates.* New York: Harcourt, 2007.

Woolley, Hannah. *The Gentlewomans Companion or, A Guide to the Female Sex; The Complete Text from 1675.* Devon, Great Britain: Prospect Books, 2001.

Zacks, Richard. *The Pirate Hunter.* New York: Hyperion, 2002.

Zimmerman, Jean. *The Women of the House.* New York: Harcourt, 2006.

Index